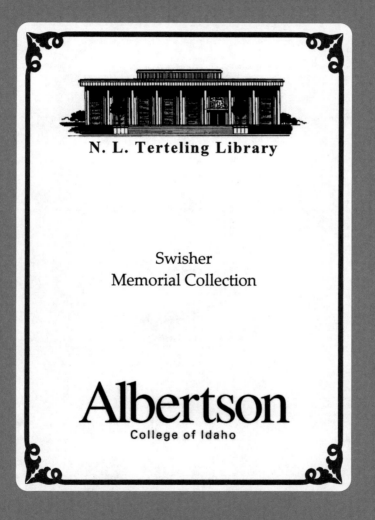

Emerson as Poet

"What a poet he was, in prose and verse!"
Robert Frost

Olympian bards who sung
Divine ideas below,
Which always find us young,
And always keep us so.
Emerson, in a verse epigraph
to the essay "The Poet"

"Always the seer is a sayer. Somehow his dream
is told; somehow he publishes it with solemn joy;
sometimes with pencil on canvas, sometimes with
chisel on stone, sometimes in towers and aisles
of granite, his soul's worship is builded; sometimes
in anthems of indefinite music; but clearest and
most permanent in words."
Emerson, in The Divinity School
Address

Emerson as Poet

Hyatt H. Waggoner

Princeton University Press

Copyright © 1974 by Princeton University Press
All Rights Reserved
Library of Congress Cataloging in Publication Data will
be found on the last printed page of this book
This book has been composed in Linotype Baskerville
Printed in the United States of America
by Princeton University Press,
Princeton, New Jersey

for Austin Warren *and* Bruno Franek

Contents

Acknowledgments

Thanks to Louise, without whom the book would not have been written; to Barton St. Armand, Austin Warren, and Joseph Yokelson, who read the work in typescript and made many helpful suggestions; and to the John Simon Guggenheim Memorial Foundation for the fellowship which gave me the time to do the necessary reading and thinking, and part of the writing.

Passages from *Poetry, Language, Thought,* by Martin Heidegger, translated by Alfred Hofstadter, copyright 1971 by Martin Heidegger, are quoted by permission of Harper & Row, Publishers; quotations from *The Imperial Self,* by Quentin Anderson, copyright 1971 by Quentin Anderson, are by permission of Alfred A. Knopf, Inc.

A Note on the Texts Used

For Emerson's published prose works, I have used the Standard Library Edition, referred to in my notes as *Works*, followed by a volume number and page or pages. For the early verse discussed in Chapter Two, I have used *The Journals and Miscellaneous Notebooks of Ralph Waldo Emerson*, ed. Gilman *et al.*, Cambridge, Harvard University Press, 1960ff., abbreviated in my notes to *JMN*. For Emerson's verse published during his lifetime or a few years after his death, I have used the Centenary Edition and referred to the volume simply as *Poems*.

Preface

Like most prefaces, this one is written last, after the book is finished and I can see what I have done, or at least have tried to do.

The impetus for it, long before I knew what shape the book might take, sprang from my growing realization that though I had argued for Emerson's "centrality" in our poetry in my 1968 *American Poets, From the Puritans to the Present*, I had let that argument rest too much on Emerson's demonstrable importance to later poets, not only of course Whitman and Dickinson but still later poets as dissimilar from him and from each other as E. A. Robinson, Robert Frost, E. E. Cummings, and, indirectly through Whitman, William Carlos Williams. With Emerson's poetry itself I had done very little more than suggest that a fresh reading of it would reveal unsuspected riches, more fine poems than the few repeatedly anthologized.

So I read his collected poems again myself, several times, and read most of what critics and literary historians of the past had said about him as a poet. I decided that with the chief exceptions of the poets themselves who had responded to his work and a few maverick critics like Alfred Kreymborg and Ludwig Lewisohn, the critics, particularly the most respectable academic critics, had very often approached the poems with inappropriate expectations in mind. This was the reason, perhaps, why the defenders of Emerson's verse and the more numerous detractors of it never seemed to be answering each other. They were not agreeing on paradigms.

The Introduction of the book that resulted from this immersion in Emerson and his critics offers a survey of past criticism of Emerson as a poet, together with some reflections, prompted by reading the critics, on why people read

poetry and how critics judge it. Since critics of the more
distant past had failed to agree on Emerson's achievement
as a poet and those of the recent past have been, for the
most part, conspicuously silent on the question, Chapter
One attempts a fresh consideration of how we should read
the poetry and what values we may hope to find in it. Chapter Two surveys the early verse, partly to show that Emerson did not, as so many critics have thought, innately lack
a talent for "correct" traditional versifying, partly to show
that when his ideas matured in the 1830's he was in effect
forced to try to forge a style of his own to express his sensibility and vision. Chapter Three returns to and amplifies
two stylistic features of the mature verse first mentioned in
Chapter One that have received little or no attention and
that ought, I think, to have a place among the expectations
we bring to it, and then examines several poems that strike
me as "middling" in quality and a number of his strongest
poems in an attempt to arrive at a just estimate of what he
achieved, granted that his verse is, as all critics have
stressed, markedly uneven in quality. Chapter Four opens
with a discussion of some of Emerson's worst failures in
verse, partly to fill the gap left by the preceding chapter,
which had said very little about his characteristic weaknesses as a poet writing in verse, partly to suggest a possible reason why, except for the years 1845-1846, he gave
more and more of his attention to prose; and then looks
closely at a few examples of the prose, finding it chiefly valuable not as philosophy, not as theory, but, at its best, as
imaginative prose-poetry of a very high order. Chapter
Five tries to draw all these threads together, emphasizing
the relations of the prose to the verse, and of content to
form, vision to voice, a problem first raised by Henry James
and most recently illuminated in essays by Carl Strauch and
R. A. Yoder.

   Looking over what I have done, I believe I have probably
raised as many questions as I have resolved, but that's all
right. There was never any idea in my mind that this might

become the definitive work on Emerson's poetry. I have said almost nothing about specific sources and have merely glanced at the relation of the poems to Emerson's changing ideas of the poet's role. With the Harvard edition of the poems not yet available, I have, except in the chapter on the childhood and youthful verse, where the evidence may be found in the *Journals and Miscellaneous Notebooks*, made no attempt to chart the development of individual poems. The list of critical and scholarly problems this book does not address itself to could be extended, but enough. They will be evident to any reader, particularly of course to those who know the poetry best. The book will have achieved its aim if its treatment of the question it does address itself to, How good a poet was Emerson? is helpful in getting the poetry, both the verse and the prose-poetry, read again, freshly and with appropriate expectations.

Emerson as Poet

A Century of Critical Agreements
and Disagreements

I take it to be a truism needing only acknowledgment that poetic reputations grow or diminish, or at least alter in character, more or less predictably in harmony with cultural changes that modify the expectations readers bring to poetry and the demands they make of it. The attempts of literary critics and philosophic aestheticians to release us from the bondage of cultural relativism and personal taste by describing the characteristics that distinguish good poetry in any age or any culture seem to me never to have proved more than temporarily and partially successful. No doubt this is because the critical systems proposed as a means of escaping cultural determinism are themselves conditioned by the culture in which they are produced. The attempt of the "New Critics" of the recent past to find an absolute standard of poetic merit was only the latest of many such attempts through Western history. Needless to say, it proved to work better with some poets, and with the poetry of some periods, than with others.

A survey of the changing styles and vocabularies used by Emerson's critics in their praise or dispraise of his poetry could be used to illustrate the difference between the culture of his day and that of our own and to remind us of the way stations between the two cultures. All literary reputations, Emerson's included, provide documentary evidence for the cultural historian to try to order. The changing reputations of minor poets seem particularly to illustrate "laws" of cultural change. We all think we can explain why Longfellow's reputation was so much greater in his lifetime than it is now: he satisfied Victorian needs and expectations, expressed their dilemmas in their language, filled a vacuum in their belief-system. Similarly, the different ways in which

Emerson's Concord neighbor Frank Sanborn and the
Freudian literary critic Ludwig Lewisohn both managed
to praise Emerson's poetry remind us of the cultural differences between the 1880's and the 1930's.

But this is not a line of thought I find myself either particularly well prepared to pursue or greatly interested in
pursuing. Someone else might follow it to fresh illuminations, but as I think about it, it seems only to illustrate what
we already know about the passing of Transcendentalism
and other cultural changes of the past century and more.
What I should like to think about instead of the changing
fashions in ways of reading Emerson's poetry are the sta-
bilities, the recognizably similar patterns of response or reaction to Emerson as a poet, and to his poetry, in his own
day and in our own—and in the period between the two.
For Emerson's poetic reputation, unlike Longfellow's
which has declined, or Very's, which has grown, has always
been a matter of dispute. It was so when he published his
first book of poems late in December of 1846 and it remains
so today. Since the assumptions and vocabularies of the dis-
putants have changed radically, how do we account for the
repetitions that persist through the changes?

In an important sense, "account for" is the wrong expression here. It seems to promise more than I have any ex-
pectation of being able to deliver. I have no hope of being
able to provide a safe refuge from the humiliating uncer-
tainties provoked by our awareness of the relativities of cultural history and the idiosyncrasies of personal taste. Still,
how shall we think about, what shall we make of, the un-
changing, or only superficially changing, judgments of
Emerson's poetry that have persisted through changing cultures? Perhaps a ray of light might be thrown on the problem if we were to take our cue from Emerson himself and
think not about cultures as such but about men and women
and their natures, particularly about the aspects of their
natures that are most relevant to the reading and evaluation
of poetry. For not all of man's psychological needs and

powers are relevant to poetry. He has sexual needs, for example, which are satisfied or not satisfied in other ways, perhaps even by pornographic fiction, but not, so far as I know, by poetry. Or again, man is a social animal, has social needs. But wolves and ants seem even more conspicuously to be social in nature, yet they do not read poetry. Despite the popularity of mass poetry readings, particularly in Russia, it seems doubtful that man's social needs play any prominent role in either the creation or the enjoyment of poetry.

But three of man's psychological, as distinguished from his biological, powers or activities are directly relevant to both the writing and the reading of poetry, and the last two of them also tend to distinguish the "humanness" of man, to set him off from animals that don't write or read poetry. To me they seem to be the feelings, particularly the aesthetic, moral, and religious feelings ("affective" states and reactions, the psychologists call them), the imagination (the psychologists' "fantasy"), and judgment (here the psychologists differ, but all would seem to agree that something real is being pointed to by the term). It will be noted that volition, the will, though traditionally considered a distinctively human activity, is not included in the list. The omission is intentional and based on several considerations. For one thing, it is not clear that what goes by the name of "will" is found only in human beings. All living things, including oysters and amoebas, seem to behave as if they have a "will" to grow, to satisfy their needs, to live. Again, despite all that has been written about the will, especially in the nineteenth century and particularly by Schopenhauer and Nietzsche, it seems to me that we really know very little about it. But most important, it seems clear that whatever it is, the will is no help toward a responsive reading of poetry. Will is directional, a "drive toward." It utilizes, seizes, incorporates, controls. A "willful" reading of poetry would presumably begin by distorting the text, violating its integrity, making it into what the will wants it to be for its own purposes. An act of will-less attention, or "intransitive attention," has to be assumed before the imagination and the feelings can respond and the judgment can operate.

Imagination, feelings, and judgment then, but not will, are and ought to be involved when we read poetry. So far as we can tell, even the higher animals do not have these powers in the way or to the degree that we do. Though at least one kind of bird and several species of mammals are tool users, they have produced no mystics and no Beethovens or Einsteins.

Imagination and feeling are paramount in the reading of and response to poetry, though judgment has its part to play, too, early as well as late. Imagination is free, creative, playful, but also, to the degree that it partakes of the qualities of fantasy, irresponsible. Feeling, when aroused by the reading of poetry, is likely to be empathic, responsive, or else not to exist at all, though possibly some poetry may arouse feelings of anger or hostility in some people. Judgment is discriminative, responsible (if we find it actually "irresponsible," we call it "poor judgment"), and dependent on what we know or think we know, on what we believe or assume regularly, on "standards" in short that permit us to judge the thing being judged. When literary judgment is evaluative and "judicial," this dependence of judgment on something other than the intrinsic nature of the object of judgment becomes particularly obvious.

Thus Arnold, though he felt that Emerson's essays were the most important prose works of the century, judged the verse to be not that of a "legitimate" poet because Arnold's reading in the British poets and the ancient classic authors had led him to form a standard of legitimacy which Emerson's poetry seemed not to satisfy. He judged prematurely, I think, not allowing his imagination and feelings to respond nonjudgmentally to the verses before him. Thus Eliot in "Sweeney Erect" dismissed Emerson as naive. The judgment was perhaps a more or less fair one if the assumptions on which it was based are true, that is, if, as Eliot had learned from Babbitt and others, Idealism, Romanticism, and lack of respect for Original Sin are fallacies. Thus the "New Critics" found Emerson's poetry inferior by their standard, which demanded that the rhetoric of good poetry reflect the ironies, ambiguities, and discontinuities of life itself as they saw it. Thus Yvor Winters, classicist and rationalistic moralist by conviction, was true to his principles when, detecting the Dionysian and ecstatic elements in Emerson, he condemned the man as a dangerous sentimentalist and consigned the works to oblivion. Thus Quentin Anderson more recently, correctly identifying the anti-authoritarian and antinomian elements in Emerson's thought, goes on to find Emerson, along with the equally "egocentric" Whitman and James, responsible for the breakdown of respect for authority and tradition among today's youth. The assumption supporting Anderson's judgment is clear: tradition, order, hierarchy, and authority are essential to civilized living. Since Emerson undermines these, he is a dangerous writer.

The evaluations just cited have all been "judgmental" in the common negative sense of the word, which may suggest that where judgment operates "purely," without imagination and feeling entering prominently into the evaluative process, we are more likely to judge negatively than positively. But of course favorable judgments may also be formed for reasons other than pleasurable imaginative and emotional responses to literary works, for reasons that involve different needs, assumptions, standards from those that would produce a negative judgment. I shall have more to say about this when I discuss the judgments of Emerson's chief nineteenth-century admirers. For now, just one illustration for the sake of clarity.

The eminent British physicist John Tyndall, who was just sufficiently younger than Emerson so that when he was maturing in the 1840's Emerson's fame had already begun to reach England, professed a lifelong interest in and admiration of Emerson's work, particularly it would seem the po-

etry. Though there is no reason to question his own statements that he enjoyed and valued the poetry, and thus in
his own way was responding to it authentically, still one
may wonder to what extent the high valuation he placed on
it was influenced by the fact that he found it reassuring precisely where he needed reassurance. The Newtonian "classical" physics of Tyndall's day appeared to demand the
materialist metaphysic that Whitehead analyzed and disposed of in *Science and the Modern World* nearly half a
century ago now. The scientist's job was to collect, describe,
and arrange "facts," conceived of as wholly independent of
him and his purposes and even of his methods. The facts
dealt with by physicists were not simply "real" among other
realities, the results of asking particular questions about
particular relationships: they were thought to be constitu-
tive, determinative, the bedrock facts of the ultimate "objective reality."

Philosophers of science were quick to draw the obvious
conclusion: one could classify the varied phenomena of human experience according to their closeness to or distance
from this "objective reality." A three-fold classification beginning with the indubitably real and moving to the subjective and perhaps merely imaginary was widely accepted
and proclaimed. The "primary" qualities of mass and energy
were "real," "secondary" qualities like color and scent
were at least partly subjective or epiphenomenal, and thus
less "real," and "tertiary" qualities like beauty and justice were wholly subjective and so completely "immaterial"
in both senses of the word. The model of the "real" universe
was that of a pool table with the balls in motion, colliding
and rebounding according to the laws governing matter in
motion, laws the physicist was busy investigating. Credit
for discovering the model was given to the open-minded
curiosity, the persistence, and the judgment of scientists.
Imagination (the formation of hypotheses) and individual
and social needs (what questions are asked?) were not simply irrelevant to the truth-finding process that had at last

discovered this model of reality, they were positively anti-
thetical to it. Imagination was for poets, romancers, and
Transcendentalists, and human nature and society had better learn to adjust itself to the realities of the pool table
world.[1]

Both the model and the ideas about how it was known—
the ontology and the epistemology—were of course inimical
not simply to organized or institutional religion with its
Biblical cosmology and its literal reading of the creation
stories in Genesis but to any religious or idealistic outlook,
any teleological view. The battle over Darwinism was
a tempest in a teapot by comparison. One might, toward the
end of the century, read and be convinced by Andrew
Dickson White's monumental study, *A History of the War-
fare of Science with Theology in Christendom*, which described with unnecessary fullness the battles religion had
always lost and science always won, and yet, having discarded all the clearly untenable doctrines and dogmas, still
remain "religious." But if one courageously pondered the
supposed implications of nineteenth-century physics, he
would find it very difficult not to conclude that *any* religious understanding of life and the cosmos, even one
friendly toward science and with so clear a humanistic
emphasis as Emerson's, was simply false.

Tyndall was unwilling to accept any such conclusions and

---

[1] The classic description of the supposed implications of Newtonian
physics is still that of A. N. Whitehead in *Science and the Modern
World*. For a contemporary view of the history of the natural sciences,
with emphasis on the discontinuities introduced by major scientific
advances, see Thomas S. Kuhn, *The Structure of Scientific Revolutions*,
The University of Chicago Press, 1970, Second Edition. Kuhn's analysis
offers support for Emerson's and Tyndall's view that imagination plays
an important role in scientific discovery. For a statement of the recipro-
cal relation between knowing and the known, implied but not developed by Kuhn, see Ruth Nanda Anshen's remarkable restatement and
expansion of the idea expressed by Emerson in "Circles" as "So to be is
so to know" in "Credo Perspectives: Their Meaning and Function," in
Paul Tillich, *My Search for Absolutes*, New York, Simon & Schuster,
1969, pp. 9-18.

10   Introduction

found in Emerson the necessary support for his position.[2]
After hearing Emerson lecture in 1847 he immediately
bought and read all his books. Emerson came to seem to
him the "noblest soul" he knew, a soul whose works had inspired in his heart "a new vigor" and fresh courage. Perhaps inspired by the custom of the devout of starting the
day with Scripture reading, he "made it a habit to begin his
daily tasks with a reading of the poems."[3] He found it immensely refreshing to read a poet in whose work science
and poetry did not appear to be speaking about different
universes, as seemed to him to be true of the work of so
many poets of his time. Emerson, he believed, was "a profoundly religious man who is really and entirely undaunted
by the discoveries of science, present, past, or prospective;
one by whom scientific conceptions are continually transmuted into the finer forms and warmer hues of an ideal
world."[4] In his scientific writings he frequently quoted "the
brave Emerson" to clarify his points. Emerson seems to
have served him as validator of two of his basic convictions,
that whatever the pool-table model of reality might seem
to require us to believe, reality is teleological (he made his
point by quoting Emerson's "the atoms march in tune" from
"Monadnoc") and the imagination is noetic, even, or perhaps especially, in science itself, where, contrary to expec-
tation, it turns out to be, he thought, "the mightiest instrument of the physical discoverer."[5]

[2] Raychel A. Haugrud, "Tyndall's Interest in Emerson," *American
Literature*, 41 (January, 1970), 507-517.

[3] *Ibid.*, 507.

[4] O. B. Frothingham, *Transcendentalism in New England*, G. P. Putnam, 1876, pp. 214-215; New York, Harper, 1959 ("Torchbook Edition"), pp. 214-215.

[5] Haugrud, p. 515. Tyndall's thinking on this matter anticipated contemporary understanding of the nature of revolutionary scientific advance. We are told, for example, that the divisions of the benzene ring
and the periodic table came in dreams. See Thomas S. Kuhn, *The
Structure of Scientific Revolutions*. Tyndall's view of the implications
of Emerson's thought for an understanding of scientific advance was

Not being a literary man with pre-formed ideas about the qualities necessary to good poetry, Tyndall did not feel Arnold's reluctant compulsion to judge Emerson's poetry inferior on aesthetic grounds. For him it was sufficient that, reading it, he felt himself in the presence of one who was, as Arnold had emphasized, "a friend and aider" of those "who would live in the spirit." His strongest tribute to Emerson is likely to strike us today as overstated, but it is worth quoting as a revelation of the kind of response Emerson's work aroused in the man Tyndall, who worked professionally as a physicist: "Whatever I have done, the world owes to him."[6] In Tyndall's judgment, Emerson's work conveyed a message he and the world of his time greatly needed. It is not clear to me that Arnold's judgment that Emerson's poetry failed to meet the specifications of all good poetry must be taken more seriously than Tyndall's less "literary" approval, even though Arnold cited literary grounds for his decision. Of the two judgments, Tyndall's seems to have sprung from a personal response to the work, Arnold's, in part at least, from impatience with a poetic aim and manner unfamiliar to him, as his finding "The Titmouse" obscure seems to suggest. Tyndall at any rate judged in a way that would have satisfied the request Wordsworth had made of his reader, "that in judging these Poems, he would decide by his own feelings genuinely."

If Tyndall's enthusiastic response to Emerson strikes us as somewhat suspect because it seems too obviously to reflect the "message-hunting" approach to literature we have all been taught to reject, still it is not clear that Whitman's or

based on inferences drawn by Tyndall long before Emerson explicitly stated his ideas in "Poetry and Imagination." In substance Emerson agreed with Tyndall: "Science does not know its debt to imagination." See *Works*, VIII, p. 16 and *passim*.

[6] Ralph L. Rusk, *The Life of Ralph Waldo Emerson*, New York, Columbia University Press, 1949, p. 457.

E. A. Robinson's or Robert Frost's responses were any less
tainted by the intrusion of extra-literary concerns. Tyndall's
response is perhaps only more frankly extra-literary. Nearly all Emerson's later admirers have conspicuously failed
even to attempt to answer the strictly literary demerits attributed to the verse by its detractors. With minor exceptions like Frank Sanborn's and John Burroughs' attempts to
answer Arnold,[7] the most ardent admirers and the most
severe detractors have tended to ignore each other, leaving
to the scholarly producers of the literary histories the task
of trying to mediate between the two positions, a task for
which most of them appear to have been ill equipped.
When, as they commonly have, the admirers have admitted
the "technical flaws," they have generally found them out-
weighed not by other aesthetic or formal merits but by the
"wisdom," while the detractors who have granted the "wisdom" have pointed out that poems are, after all, works of
art, so that if the wisdom must be judged ill-expressed, no
amount of it can change a poor poem into a good one.

If all authentic literary response is personal, involving the
imagination, feelings, and judgment of the reader, as I have
argued, then this curious situation becomes perhaps a little
less hard to understand. Still, the lack of debate over spe-
cifics that characterizes more than a century of Emerson
criticism does seem to need some explaining. Poe's achievement in his poetry, for example, has been from the beginning and still is a matter of controversy, but the point is
that whether we ought to assent to Emerson's dismissal of
Poe as "that jingle man" or judge him our greatest poet has
been debated, with charges made and answered—and then

[7] F. B. Sanborn, "Emerson Among the Poets," in *The Genius and
Character of Emerson: Lectures at the Concord School of Philosophy*,
ed. F. B. Sanborn, Boston, Houghton Mifflin, 1898, pp. 173-214. (Original edition, Boston, James R. Osgood, 1885.) John Burroughs, "Arnold's
View of Emerson and Carlyle," *Indoor Studies*, Boston, Houghton Mifflin, 1889, pp. 128-161. Burroughs returned to the subject in "Flies in
Amber" in *The Last Harvest*, Boston, Houghton Mifflin, 1922, pp. 86-
102.

of course remade. Similarly, the rejection of Whitman by
the majority of readers in his century has elicited a small
library of critical defenses in ours, defenses which at first
tended to fall back on generalized approval of the man and
his message but in recent decades have often addressed
themselves to the specific charges of earlier detractors, particularly to the blanket charge that his verse is "formless,"
finding coherence in "Song of Myself," for example, method
and meaning in seemingly random catalogues, and suggestions of prosodic patterns where there had seemed to be
only chaos. Not so with Emerson, for some reason. With the
principal exceptions of Carl Strauch and, most recently,
R. A. Yoder, the chief Emersonians of recent years have addressed themselves to other matters, to Emerson's ideas and
sources, for example. Whicher found the poetry defective
but hinted that as criticism develops, we may see more in
it and find ways of defending it. Rusk remains above the
battle, content with the facts. The story of Emerson's reputation as a poet forms a curious chapter in our literary history, a chapter so peculiar in some respects that it may be
profitable to examine it in some detail.

Response, reaction, reputation. Response is personal and
based on the particular work, or on one's sense of "the man"
behind all the works. A strongly positive response signifies
that specific works, or the tenor of the whole body of works
("the man behind the work"), has given pleasure or filled a
need. Response can be personal and authentic without being "purely aesthetic," if any strong response to literature
ever is. This was Ludwig Lewisohn's point when, defending Emerson in the 1930's, he said that modern readers are
likely to approach literature not as "an elegant diversion or
an illustration of the foreknown and fixed" but as "moral
research," a search for truth and meaning[8]—a definition of
an approach that looks back to Emerson and forward to

[8] Ludwig Lewisohn, *Expression in America*, New York, Harper, 1932,
p. ix. (In later printings, the title of the work was changed to *The
Story of American Literature*.)

Wallace Stevens at once. Assuming, like D. H. Lawrence, that this is the way literature *should* be read, Lewisohn finds that Emerson wrote a sufficient number of poems that will stand the test of time, for each later age will "by some instinctive and passionate reinterpretation" make them its own.[9] "Instinctive and passionate reinterpretation" is highly personal and thus not easy to predict, but it is likely to be instructive, leading us toward some real quality in the work being responded to.

Reaction is more predictable just because it is less personal. It was as predictable that registrants at the Concord School of Philosophy should value Emerson as a poet as that the New Critics in their heyday should not value him. Neither group needed very much contact with the poetry itself to form its judgment. Nor did Vernon Parrington or V. F. Calverton when they came to write their histories of our literature. Parrington ignores the poetry and Calverton dismisses it; neither gives any evidence of having given it a chance to speak to him. Their reactions were predictable, given their outlooks and preoccupations. Evidence of a true response, even one that finally issued in detailed negative judgments, with reasons, would have been very surprising in the books they wrote. Reactions, as I am using the word, naturally tend toward the mechanical and determined.

Reputations, high or low, are often maintained for years for reasons that seem quite analogous to what physicists mean by "inertia." A writer's reputation may be high or low among those who have never read a word of his work, and literary historians, who help to perpetuate or to alter reputations, often seem to have read each other's works more carefully than those of the writers they are treating. As we move from response to reaction to reputation we are moving away from the work of art itself. For nearly a half-century now, Emerson's reputation as a poet has been in general low, but it is not clear to what extent that low repu-

9 *Ibid.*, p. 136. Cf. Lawrence's *Studies in Classic American Literature*, New York, Thomas Seltzer, 1923, p. 254 and *passim*; New York, The Viking Press, 1961 (paperback), p. 171 and *passim*.

tation reflects the lack of response, or negative responses, of actual readers of the poems themselves. There have been many reasons in the recent past why a person might have held Emerson's poetry in low esteem without having read very much of it, even without having read it at all.

While Emerson was alive and for some years later, the difficulty of relating reputation to response was complicated in a quite different way. Emerson the man was held in such high respect that even those who really did not enjoy the verse very much generally stated their reservations about it as gently as possible or not at all. Emerson was, after all, by common consent our most eminent man of letters. He who had issued America's declaration of literary independence had demonstrated, in the eyes of his many European admirers, what form that independence would take. Americans still smarting from European charges of cultural barrenness would think twice about becoming detractors of their prize European exhibit.

Furthermore, Emerson the man on the platform and in more intimate contact seems to have made a powerfully positive impression on almost everyone. He seemed saintly, courageous, wise—wise even to those who confessed they were not sure they fully understood what he was saying. If today's journalists were reporting one of his lectures, they would probably describe the speaker as "charismatic."[10]

[10] The impression made by Emerson on the lecture platform is reported in many first-hand accounts and is the subject of a number of scholarly studies. See, for example, J. R. Lowell, "Emerson the Lecturer," *Works*, Boston, Houghton Mifflin, 1892, pp. 349-360; also, *Letters of James Russell Lowell*, C. E. Norton, ed., New York, Harper, 1894, II, 275-276; O. W. Holmes, *Emerson*, Boston, Houghton Mifflin, 1885, pp. 374-379; Cabot's *Memoir*, vol. II, *passim* (Emerson's *Works*, XIV); Frank B. Sanborn, *Ralph Waldo Emerson*, Boston, Small, Maynard, 1901, pp. 123-127; Charles Ives, *Essays Before a Sonata*, New York, W. W. Norton, 1964, p. 35; John Jay Chapman, *Emerson and Other Essays*, New York, AMS Press, 1965 (reprint of the 1899 edition), p. 33; and Rusk, *Life, passim*. Writing in 1900, Santayana opened his great appreciative essay on Emerson by noting the difficulty of achieving objective judgment of the work of a man of Emerson's charisma. See "Emerson," *Interpretations of Poetry and Religion*.

Emerson became both an institution and a symbol in his own lifetime, so much so that the later part of the century might well be called "the age of Emerson."[11] "The sage of Concord," "the seer of Concord," "the wisest American": no wonder Frank Sanborn opened his attempted refutation of Arnold's charges by saying to the assembled students at the Concord School of Philosophy, "I wish to speak of Emerson, and not merely of a poet; for to me he was a poet and much more."[12] He explained what he meant in a way that at once is typical of nineteenth-century laudatory criticism of Emerson as a poet and yet seems to me to retain its hold on some kind of truth:

> Had the Concord seer never written a line of verse, he would still have been a poet by virtue of that insight, that clairvoyance of the imagination, which is the one indispensable token of poetic power.[13]

Emerson's reputation as a poet—and not simply as a man gifted with poetic power—grew as his international reputation as a sage grew. The reviewers of his first volume (*Poems*, 1847) mostly reacted to finding in the poems the opinions, particularly the religious opinions, they had already accepted or rejected in the lectures and essays. The rejecters seem to have been in the majority. Poe gave qualified praise to several poems but prefaced it by placing Emerson among "a class of gentlemen with whom we have no patience whatever—the mystic for mysticism's sake."[14] Francis Bowen registered his objections to Emerson's opinions at some length, then briefly dismissed the poems as "prosaic and unintelligible."[15] Orestes Brownson made no

[11] As Paul Elmer More wrote long ago, to speak of the late nineteenth century as "the age of Emerson" is not necessarily to offer unqualified praise.
[12] Sanborn, "Emerson Among the Poets," p. 173.
[13] *Ibid.*, p. 174.
[14] A. H. Quinn, *Edgar Allan Poe: A Critical Biography*, New York, D. Appleton, 1941, p. 328.
[15] Rusk, *Life*, p. 323.

attempt to disguise his religious reaction as an aesthetic response: the poems were, he said, not "sacred chants" but "hymns to the devil."[16] Only Lowell, writing in *A Fable for Critics* the following year, seems clearly to be attempting to respond to the verse rather than to Emerson's reputation or to his opinions, and his judgment is negative: though the poems contain "mines of rich matter" (unrefined ore? potential poetry?), they are incoherent. We must look to the prose, he thought, for Emerson's best poetry.[17] The pleasure Longfellow found in *Poems* when the work was read aloud to him he confided to his diary, in terms that leave it questionable how much he understood of what he had heard.[18] Holmes is said to have reacted negatively at first, though by the time he wrote his biographical and critical study after Emerson's death he was ready to give the poems a sympathetic and discriminating reading. But by this time of course Emerson's reputation was at its height and there were few public detractors of anything he had written.

Among his late-century admirers particularly, the man still overshadowed the verse, as his disciple John Burroughs, speaking for many, would soon make clear in several

[16] *Ibid.*

[17] As late as 1883 Lowell seems not to have essentially altered his opinion of the verse, though he was now prepared to admit that occasional single lines were fine. Replying to a correspondent who had invited his opinion of Emerson's work after the latter's death, he wrote, "As for Emerson's verse (though he has written some [verses, i.e., lines] as exquisite as any in the language) I suppose we must give it up. That he had a sense of the higher harmonies of language no one that ever heard him lecture can doubt. The structure of his prose, as one listened to it, was as nobly metrical as the King James version of the Old Testament, and this made it all the more puzzling that he should have been absolutely insensitive to the harmony of verse. For it was there he failed—single verses are musical enough." (*Letters*, C. E. Norton, ed., II, 275)

[18] Edward Wagenknecht, *Longfellow*, New York, Longmans Green, 1955, p. 25. (The poems, read aloud to Longfellow, "gave us," he wrote in his journal, "the keenest pleasure; though many of the pieces present themselves Sphinx-like. . . .")

essays on the master who had influenced him so powerfully. Bowing in 1889 to the justice of the detractions earliest enunciated by Lowell and most recently elaborated by the prestigious Arnold, Burroughs felt obliged to admit that "a poet on the usual terms we must admit Emerson was not. He truly had a Druidical cast. His song is an incantation. . . . His verse is full of disembodied poetic values."[19] He tried to clarify the thought behind this last rather mysterious sentence by saying,

> We go to him as we go to a fountain to drink. . . . [We] need his moral and spiritual tonics. . . . We live in a sick age, and he has saved the lives of many of us.[20]

To its admirers, the poetry, in short, whatever its faults as verse might be, could be read as gospel, as the good news capable of saving perishing men. When one approached it as Scripture, the literary flaws seemed unimportant, the prophet and his message reducing to insignificance the failures of expression. The man, the mind, the vision loomed larger than any of the works, not simply larger than the "imperfect" verse but larger than the prose too: "When I think of Emerson," Burroughs admitted as he moved toward the end of his lengthy answer to Arnold's charges, "I think of him as a man, not as an author; it was his rare and charming personality that healed us and kindled our love."[21] Years later, he would express the same response while making the judgment explicit: "I cherish and revere the name of Emerson so profoundly, and owe him such a debt, that it seems, after all, a pity to point out the flaws in his precious amber."[22]

Among the half dozen books and dozens of briefer treatments devoted to Emerson in the two decades following his death in 1882, two stand out as defining the issues facing

---

[19] *Indoor Studies*, pp. 151-152.   [20] *Ibid.*, p. 154.
[21] *Ibid.*   [22] *The Last Harvest*, p. 102.

Emerson's critics then and since. Both of them express very personal and strongly positive responses to "Emerson," the man who may be discerned in and behind his works, and both also express some judicial reservations about the works themselves. Henry James briefly and obliquely in a review of Cabot's *Memoir* reprinted in *Partial Portraits* and John Jay Chapman at length and directly in *Emerson and Other Essays* felt Emerson to be immensely important to them but judged his achievement as a writer to be problematical.

James talks chiefly about Emerson the man and the lecturer, more briefly about the prose writer, without mentioning specifically the poetry as such. The book before him for review, chiefly an evocation of the man who had produced the writings, gave him the excuse he wanted to dwell upon the looming figure of the man rather than upon the flawed works. Emerson and James's Swedenborgian father had been friendly theological opponents, with Emerson achieving worldwide fame while the father remained an obscure eccentric. James found himself at once very little interested in the metaphysical and theological differences that had separated Emerson and his father and very much aware of the extent to which between them they had expressed and helped to shape the world of his youth, a much simpler world as it seemed to him. So he focused on Emerson and the age of Emerson, throwing in a few tentative observations on the matter that he himself as a writer was chiefly concerned with, the matter of form. Emerson seemed to James to have expressed himself chiefly in the lecture and the essay, but were not these modes of expression so very personal as to be in effect formless? Revering Emerson as he did, James could touch only lightly on aesthetic questions.

Still, several of his off-handedly delivered judgments are quite as relevant to the verse as they are to the prose, and one of them at least seems to me to be more relevant to the verse than to the essays. After admitting that "other writers have arrived at a more complete expression" and illustrating by saying that "Wordsworth and Goethe, for instance, give one a sense of having found their form," James admits what we can only suppose he would have found a major aesthetic flaw in any writer who had engaged his feelings and imagination less fully. Emerson's difference from such writers as Wordsworth and Goethe, he says, is that "with Emerson we never lose the sense that he is still seeking it," that is, his proper form.

Nevertheless, James feels, Emerson retains his "singular power" over us because

> he is a striking exception to the general rule that writings live in the last resort by their form; that they owe a large part of their fortune to the art with which they have been composed. It is hardly too much, or too little, to say of Emerson's writings in general that they were not composed at all.[23]

As I shall argue, it seems to me that Emerson's writings were "composed," that in his best poems and essays he did "find his form," but James's remarks seem not wholly wide of the mark, even so. The nineteenth-century "personal essay," exploiting subjectivity, seemed to James to make too few demands on the writer to deserve to be called a literary "form," and as for the poems, it seems to me true that Emerson did not regularly, consistently succeed in finding the form best suited to his intentions and meanings. When James grants Emerson's writings importance even though they were not "composed," he is suggesting a distinction between *Dichter* and poet that still seems worth thinking about. When he says that we sense in Emerson's work that he is "seeking" a form, he is anticipating the judgment of the many recent scholar-critics, who—with whatever unfairness to Emerson—find in Whitman's poetry the fulfillment of the ideal Emerson could announce but not himself achieve.

Many of the important questions about Emerson's value to us as a writer, and particularly as a poet, not raised by

[23] *Partial Portraits*, London, Macmillan, 1888, pp. 9, 32.

James's brief remarks were raised by Chapman a decade later. Like James, though for different reasons, Chapman was deeply engaged with his subject. As Sherman Paul has recently reminded us, Emerson and Garrison were Chapman's "heroes of conscience." In college Chapman had been, in his own words, "intoxicated with Emerson," and he always remained grateful to the poet-seer for the help he had received. When he came to write his long essay he had some sharp criticisms to make of his hero, the severity of which Sherman Paul has explained this way:

> Chapman's criticism of Emerson was severe not simply because the seer lost power by not acting, but because Emerson had become profoundly a part of himself. No one ever gave himself over so entirely to Emerson as Chapman did. Speaking of his "rag-dolls" (Emerson and Goethe), Chapman recalls that he found his Emerson "in an old family trunk" and that long ago he began "to shows signs of wear and tear."[24]

But even after the inspirer of his youth had come to seem insufficient, Chapman could still say, "I can't imagine what I should have been if it hadn't been for Emerson." His essay then represents in the highest degree a personal response that becomes the enabling condition of some of the shrewdest judgments of Emerson ever made. As Sherman Paul once again has put it, "What he said of Emerson can be said of him: 'Open his works at hazard. You hear a man talking.' "[25]

Though he is chiefly concerned with Emerson's prose, Chapman opens up the subject of Emerson's achievement as a poet as no one before him had. Acknowledging the lack of agreement about the merits of the verse, he finds it ironic that the poetry of a man "whose main thesis was that piety is a crime" should have elicited piety in its defenders. He

[24] "The Identities of John Jay Chapman," in *Transcendentalism and Its Legacy*, Simon and Parsons, ed., Ann Arbor, The University of Michigan Press, 1966, pp. 143-144.
[25] *Ibid.*, p. 140.

agrees with those who find the poetry cold ("His tempera-
ture is below blood-heat") and admits that Emerson is generally at his best in "happy and golden lines, snatches of
grace." The defects the critics have found are real, and "lovers of Emerson's poems freely acknowledge all these defects, but find in them another element . . . the mystical
element." Far more than the work of most poets, Emerson's
poems, he believes, have the effect of creating "an opening
of the reader's mind." Though the poems "are overshadowed by the greatness of his prose, . . . they are authentic."

Chapman has a good deal more to say about the verse
that is still worth hearing, but three of the points he makes
about Emerson as a writer of both prose and verse seem to
me especially significant. First, Emerson is not in any important sense a "thinker" (that is, a philosopher: "He discovered nothing; he bears no relation whatever to the history of philosophy.") but a "poet-preacher" and "a great
artist." An artist must capture the reader's "virgin attention," and Chapman submits that "Nobody has the knack of
this more strongly than Emerson in his prose writings." Second, Emerson is a better artist in his prose than he is in his
verse. The statement just quoted about Emerson's ability
to capture the reader's "virgin attention" is followed by the
admission, "But he cannot do it in verse." All Chapman's
praise for Emerson's artistry is reserved for his prose style,
as when he speaks of the "extraordinary beauty of language" of *Nature*, which he describes as "a supersensuous,
lyrical, and sincere rhapsody." Finally, Emerson as a poetic
artist in both verse and prose is "authentic" even when, as
usually in his verse, he is not great, for his style is a natural
outgrowth of his special heritage and his particular time
and place. Even as a writer of the verses that Chapman
finds poetically inferior to the prose, we should conclude
that "Here is no defective English poet . . . but an American
poet." Both in prose and in verse, though most remarkably
in the prose, "His style is American, and beats with the
pulse of the climate. He is the only writer we have had who

writes as he speaks, who makes no literary parade, has no pretensions of any sort."[26]

As we shall see, it would take most of the literary historians and critics of Emerson a half-century or more to catch up with some of the insights that emerged from Chapman's passionate engagement with his subject in the closing years of the last century.

Reading James and Chapman, we feel that they posed the right questions, that their discussions of Emerson do not need to be "explained" by reference to the time of composition. But when we turn to the lesser critics we have to keep reminding ourselves that at the time of his death "The seer of Concord" was indisputably America's best-known and most revered man of letters, with admirers and even disciples abroad as well as at home. In England, Germany, and France, particularly, his following was, or soon would be, large and devoted, including types as varied as the poet Alfred Noyes, the philologists Jakob and Wilhelm Grimm, the philosopher Friedrich Nietzsche, and the playwright Maurice Maeterlinck. Memories of the man, intimate like those of Sanborn or gained only from seeing and hearing him lecture, were still alive and often formed the valuable core of a rapidly growing library of Emersoniana. Readers abroad delighted in his difficulties for them, finding in them the virtue of a distinctively American quality. At home he was credited with the rapid growth of Christian Science, though Mary Baker Eddy denied any personal debt, and it was increasingly clear that he had done more than anyone else to create a climate favorable to the flourishing of both the Ethical Culture Society and liberal Protestantism. With "Browning Societies" springing up everywhere to facilitate understanding of the spiritual message of the British poet, the wonder is that there were apparently no Emerson so-

[26] "Emerson" in *Emerson and Other Essays*, pp. 3-108, *passim*, esp. 83-96, on the verse.

cieties, though the Concord School of Philosophy was one in effect. Still, Concord's celebration of the centenary of his birth was a national event. Many notables gathered to honor the sage and hear William James describe him as the American who had most fully embodied and expressed all that was best and most original in our national character and thought. Like Santayana before him and Dewey later, James felt that this thinker who had scorned systematic reasoning had yet made a major, perhaps the major, contribution to American philosophy. With James's voice added to that of his novelist brother, the naturalists John Muir and John Burroughs, and the brilliantly eccentric reformer Chapman and the composer Charles Ives, there was an almost unmixed chorus of praise in the several decades following Emerson's death.

Naturally the veneration accorded the seer affected judgments of the achievement of his verse. Joel Benton led the way in 1883 with a treatment of the prophetic aspect of the verse that managed to be at once enthusiastic and intelligent.[27] The following year Sanborn defended the master's craftsmanship ("he purposely roughened his verse")[28] as well as his vision, and the next year E. C. Stedman, himself a minor conventional poet as well as a critic whose perceptiveness has not been sufficiently acknowledged, judged

[27] *Emerson As a Poet*, New York, M. Holbrook, 1883. Benton "led the way" among those who wrote of Emerson as poet after his death, but G. W. Cooke's chapter on the poetry in his *Ralph Waldo Emerson: His Life, Writings, and Philosophy*, Boston, James R. Osgood, 1881, which had appeared while Emerson still lived, had offered a thorough and in many ways perceptive treatment, finding Emerson's models not among any of his contemporaries but among the Elizabethan and Metaphysical poets whose verse Cooke found Emerson's resembling. Cooke's chapter, as I see it, continues to have more suggestive value than any but a small handful of the later treatments. Cooke was a sympathetic and attentive reader of the verse, and he did not suppose that the poetic conventions of the nineteenth century were the only legitimate ones.

[28] *The Genius and Character of Emerson*, p. 211.

Emerson a "great" poet, great in the phrase, the line, the quatrain, despite the awkwardness of much of his verse and the fact that he could seldom sustain his longer poems. Stedman's *Poets of America* was an important book by an influential literary figure. If Emerson had lived to read its treatment of his poetry, I suspect he would particularly have liked what Stedman had to say about the special quality of the "vision" in the verse:

> I am not sure but one must be of the poet's own country and breeding to look quite down his vistas and by-paths: for every American has something of Emerson in him, and the secret of the land was in the poet. . . .[29]

In the same year, 1885, Holmes's biographical and critical study of his friend appeared in the "American Men of Letters" series. Its chapter on the poetry is at once appreciative and discriminating, sympathetic and reserved. With his strong belief, both in theory and practice, in neoclassical principles of art and his temperamental distrust of mysticism, Holmes must have found this chapter the most difficult one in the book to write. Still, he manages, though with a suggestion of embarrassment at times, not only to find a good many poems to praise but to declare that at its best the verse, however uneven, concentrates and distills the meanings of the essays. But after he has said as much as he can for it, he ends not far from the position of Sanborn and Burroughs: Emerson's "fascination" as a poet, he thinks, is not really to be explained except as the effect of his "serene, high, pure intelligence and moral nature." It is finally this, not his art, that makes him "infinitely precious to us."[30]

The combination of Holmes's reputation with the early

[29] E. C. Stedman, *Poets of America*, Boston, Houghton Mifflin, 1885, pp. 158-159.

[30] Oliver Wendell Holmes, *Ralph Waldo Emerson*, Boston, Houghton Mifflin, 1885, chap. XIV, "Emerson's Poems," pp. 310-342. The quotations are from pp. 341 and 342.

date of his book appears to have given it substantial influence over the writers of the studies that appeared during
the remaining years of the century. In 1888 the British critic
and biographer Richard Garnett was explicit about his in-
debtedness in his *Life of Ralph Waldo Emerson*. "The
genius of his verse," he decided, "is best characterized by
a happy phrase of Dr. Holmes's—it is elemental." Emphasizing what Holmes had reluctantly admitted, the "fitful
and fragmentary" character of Emerson's achievement as
a poet, and coming down hard on Emerson's technical in-
expertness ("The poems offend continually by lame unscan-
nable lines, and clumsinesses and obscurities of expression"), Garnett finally tipped the scales toward approval of
this "lovely, wayward child of the American Parnassus"—
who, he thought, had outdone even Wordsworth in getting
us to "participate" in Nature—by throwing into the balance
his *indigenous* quality. "But after all," he concluded, "it is
his greatest glory as a poet to have been the harbinger of
distinctively American poetry to America."[31]

Two other late-century treatments of the poetry pretty
much follow the Holmes line and were probably influenced
by his book. When the Dartmouth professor Charles F.
Richardson published his pioneering two-volume study,
American Literature, 1607-1885, in 1889, he devoted a long
chapter exclusively to Emerson's poetry. Since he intended
his work as a college textbook, much of what he has to say
is simply expository, but his judgments often seem distinguished by their aptness, or at least by their reflection of
original thought, when they are compared with those of
many of our later literary historians. For example, Richardson thinks that Emerson "was deliberate in his noblest lines
and most polished poems; he was no less deliberate in his
quaintest, most irregular, and cacophonous verses." Or
this: "It is more truthful to call him a great man who wrote

[31] Richard Garnett, *Life of Ralph Waldo Emerson*, London, Walter
Scott, 1888, pp. 130, 131, 135.

poems, than to call him a great poet." Or this, surely: "His
poetry at its best reaches heights which Longfellow or
Bryant could not attain."[32]

Katharine Lee Bates of Wellesley, better known today for
"America the Beautiful" than as the author of *American Literature* (1897), also stays pretty much within the territory
first mapped out by Holmes. Her judgment that Emerson
is *the* American writer is suggested to us before we begin
to read what she has to say of him: a portrait of the seer
forms the frontispiece of her book. Comparing him as a
poet with Bryant, Longfellow, Holmes, Whittier, and
Lowell, whose verse she has just treated, she finds them all,
despite their merits, dwarfed by greater European poets
whose work theirs resembles, while Emerson she finds *sui
generis*. In a vein more prophetic than she could guess, she
writes, "In Emerson . . . we have, if not an acknowledged
master, yet a poet whose lyricism is so strange and rare as
to defy the critics." Continuing to appear to be foreseeing
the dilemmas of many later academic literary historians
when dealing with Emerson's verse, she says, "They can
compare him to nobody, measure him by nothing, and are
sometimes driven by sheer perplexity to pronounce him not
a poet at all." Though her patriotism no doubt played a part
in creating her enthusiastic approval of Emerson's poetry
despite the "faults" which she finds "the critics" accusing
him of, which she dutifully lists, she does not list the "American" quality of his work as a value. Instead, following
Holmes rather than Garnett, she finds its "prime value" in
"the elevation of spirit it imparts."[33]

Several years earlier the prevailing chorus of praise that
tended to dominate the writing on the poems in this period
had found less emotional, more judicious expression in an
equally unpretentious little textbook that is worth quoting

[32] Charles F. Richardson, *American Literature, 1607-1885*, New York,
G. P. Putnam's Sons, 1889, p. 148.

[33] Katharine Lee Bates, *American Literature*, New York, Macmillan,
1897, pp. 167, 172.

because it anticipates a number of Emerson's more prestigious later critics even while it speaks both out of and to its own time. It was 1893 when Francis H. Underwood wrote in *The Builders of American Literature* that

> Many of . . . [Emerson's] poems are the expressions of thoughts found also in his essays. Some of his poems are of the highest beauty; others appear to have been wrought without much art. . . . "The Problem," "Each and All," and some others may be named as absolutely unsurpassed in our time. In grandeur of thought and power of expression, Emerson at his best is first of American poets.[34]

In 1904 Elizabeth Luther Cary's *Emerson: Poet and Thinker* summed up the chief points of agreement among those who had responded positively to Emerson's poetry in the two decades after his death and added a judgment of her own that Sanborn had first suggested and Richardson had repeated but that no one had yet done more than assert. In many instances at least, she maintained, the so-called faults of the verse were not only deliberate, as Sanborn had said, but not really faults at all except when measured by the wrong yardstick, virtues rather, eccentricities that worked to accomplish his purposes. Although her book makes it clear that it is really the "elevation of spirit" provided by the verse that leads her to conclude that Emerson is our greatest poet, she makes a determined if rather generalized effort *not* to apologize for his "faults" but to justify them as functionally necessary for a poet who held to an organic ideal of poetry.[35] Her arguments anticipated the point made more succinctly by Charles Ives in the form of a question he would ask in the tribute to Emerson he wrote as an explanatory preface to his Concord Sonata: "If Emerson's manner is not always beautiful in accordance with

[34] Francis H. Underwood, *The Builders of American Literature*, Boston, Lee and Shepard, 1893, p. 122.

[35] Elizabeth Luther Cary, *Emerson, Poet and Thinker*, New York, G. P. Putnam's Sons, 1904, "Poems," pp. 205-220. See esp. pp. 212ff.

accepted standards, why not accept a few other standards?"
But since she has little to say specifically about what such
"other standards" would be, we are left finally with the impression that for her too, as for Ives, Emerson was, as Ives
would put it, "greater . . . in the realms of revelation—
natural disclosure—than in those of poetry, philosophy, or
prophecy." He was for both of them, as for so many others
in these years, in Ives's words, "America's deepest ex-
plorer of the spiritual immensities" and thus important as
"a poet of natural and revealed philosophy," however fitful
and imperfect his technical control might be, or at least
seem to be.[36] Meanwhile, though neither Cary nor Ives
seems to have known it, E. P. Whipple had long since suggested some of the "other standards" that might be applied
in judging Emerson's poetry. Whipple had compared the
poetry with Wordsworth's, for example, and found that
Emerson was no imitator but an extender and enlarger,
bringing in "new materials" and new ideas. He had found
the poetry "original in the sense in which the word is applied to the recognized masters of song," and the best
of the poems not ingeniously wrought compositions but
"revelations."[37]

Whipple was a critic, Holmes a poet and doctor, Ives a
businessman and composer, Cary a professional journalist-
biographer. They could afford to be bold, but most of the
chroniclers of our literary history around the turn of the
century were more cautious. They were well aware of
Emerson's eminence and of the enthusiasm of his admirers;
but as professors of literature who were supposed to know,
if anyone did, the qualities that distinguished good poems
from bad ones, would they not be betraying their profession

[36] *Essays Before a Sonata and Other Writings by Charles Ives*, Howard
Boatwright, ed., New York, Norton, 1964, pp. 11, 13. Though not completed and published until 1920, the essay on Emerson seems to reflect
opinions and attitudes formed much earlier.

[37] E. P. Whipple, *American Literature and Other Papers*, Boston,
Ticknor, 1887, pp. 259-298.

and undermining their own authority if they argued that
"revelation" could outweigh technical faults? They felt secure when dealing with the conventional Longfellow, only
a little less secure when dealing with the unconventional
Whitman. But Emerson made them acutely uneasy with his
unconventional handling of conventional forms. Except for
Richardson and Bates, the literary historians either belittle
Emerson's poetry on technical grounds or, trying to balance
its faults and its virtues impartially, fall into incoherence.
The conservative and eminent Brander Matthews of Columbia, for example, in his textbook *Introduction to the
Study of American Literature* (1896) admitted both that
"the spirit of a true poet Emerson had abundantly" and that
his verse contained "no lack of elevation," so that now and
then his best stanzas are "bracing," well suited to "lift up
the heart of man." Nevertheless, the only poem Matthews
could honestly praise was "The Concord Hymn," an exception, he felt, to Emerson's generally "careless" and "very
slovenly" versifying. Emerson unfortunately "cared too little for form often to write so perfect a poem. The bonds of
rime and meter irked him and he broke them willfully,"
with the result, the reader is left to conclude, that however
much he may have been a poet in "spirit," he was only rarely and accidentally one in achievement.[38] In 1900 the illus-
trious Barrett Wendell in his *Literary History of America*
made even less of an effort than Matthews had to be patient
with Emerson's poetic eccentricities, describing Emerson as
a kind of "prophet" who perversely expressed his heretical
views in poems marked by an "erratic oddity of form." With
the remark that more orthodox minds would have written
them as hymns, he leaves the reader to conclude that they
are really not worth discussing as poems.[39]

Julian Abernethy's determined efforts to balance fairly

[38] Brander Matthews, *Introduction to the Study of American Literature*, New York, American Book Co., 1896, p. 103.
[39] Barrett Wendell, *A Literary History of America*, New York, Scribner's, 1900, p. 317.

the conflicting views of Emerson as a poet in his *American Literature* (1902) result in what seems at least like sheer incoherence. There is much poetry in the prose, he notes, and *Nature* might even be described as "a kind of prose poem." But with "critical opinion" of the verse so "widely varied," he can only report the virtues its admirers find in it and then add, in his own voice, that Emerson "lacked skill in . . . the technique of verse," had a "defective" ear for verse rhythms, and wrote verse lacking not only "passion or emotion" but even "human warmth and fellowship." Still, oddly enough, he felt that Emerson's "poetic limitations can be frankly admitted without detriment to his worth or fame." Whether as a prophet or as a poet he does not say.[40]

A year later W. P. Trent would come to a somewhat similar conclusion in his *A History of American Literature, 1607-1865.* If Emerson is not really a philosopher, he asks, is he a poet? Many think so, many do not. On the whole, the critics who have emphasized Emerson's weakness in technique have proved their case, Trent thinks, beyond dispute, painful as it may be to have to admit it, in view of the very real greatness pointed to by Emerson's admirers. With apparent reluctance, Trent enumerates the by now more or less standard list of faults in the verse, then, dropping the appearance of ambivalence, adds several more that he has discovered himself. Too often, he notes, Emerson tends to treat subjects that are intrinsically unfit for poetry, and when he does treat poetic subjects, he does so unpoetically, in a manner "almost entirely" lacking in "true poetic glow and flow." Not only is he unable to sustain a poem but,

[40] Julian W. Abernethy, *American Literature*, New York, Charles E. Merrill, 1902, pp. 180-182. An approach similar to Abernethy's in its effort at a judicious balancing of views but less obviously incoherent may be found in James B. Smiley's *A Manual of American Literature*, New York, American Book Co., 1905, pp. 137-139, where we may read that Emerson undoubtedly had "the soul of a poet" and sometimes, despite the technical flaws in his verse, wrote like one, expressing "the delicate perceptions and profound insight of a true lover of nature."

"Worse still, he is prone to jargon, to bathos, to lapses of taste." One might guess that Emerson's poetry had been disposed of by this point, but no. Resuming his judicious tone, Trent concludes that nevertheless, on the other hand, Emerson produced enough "genuinely fine poems and passages" to lift him "above the category of minor poets." He leaves it unclear just how bathetic a poet must be to be justly labelled as "minor."[41]

In 1907, just a quarter century after Emerson's death, George E. Woodberry's *Emerson* in the "English Men of Letters" series lifted the discussion back to something like the level it had attained in 1885 in Holmes's "American Men of Letters" volume. The chapter on the poems gives the impression that Woodberry had read and thought about them, and that some of them at least had engaged his imagination and aroused his feelings. Mingling praise and blame judiciously but with some evidence of personal involvement with his subject, Woodberry provides a balanced summation of the long debate over whether Emerson's technical "faults" or his "vision" was most important. Despite his sympathy for Emerson the man, he was inclined to think it was the former that must be emphasized, as the opening sentence of his chapter reveals: "By no means a perfect master of prose, he was much less a master of the instrument of verse." His lack of artistry was not, Woodberry felt, as some of the early uncritical admirers had said, an evidence of deliberate experimentation; rather, " . . . he was inartistic by necessity." Though "inartistic by necessity" is likely to strike us as an ambiguous phrase (What sort of "necessity"? An inappropriate intention? Defective gifts?), Woodberry quickly resolves the ambiguity by falling back on the by now familiar maneuver: a few of Emerson's poems are "admirable," but though he was by nature and intention "fundamentally a poet," he had, most unfortunately, "an imperfect faculty of expression." "Bacchus" is "perhaps his most

[41] W. P. Trent, *A History of American Literature, 1607-1865,* New York, D. Appleton, 1903, pp. 332-333.

original poem" and there is originality too in the way even his less successful verse expresses the impact of science on his imagination. This, rather than "the mystical element" Chapman had noted, is what saves the verse for Woodberry, so far as it can be saved. Clearly, Woodberry is writing in and for a new century.[42]

The views Woodberry expressed were re-expressed with only minor variations by the majority of those who wrote on Emerson's verse for the next quarter century. The collaborative product of the Cornell English department edited in 1909 by Theodore Stanton, *A Manual of American Literature*, for example, made explicit what Woodberry had only implied, that Emerson's popular reputation as "a philosophic mystic and a lay preacher" was outside the proper domain of literary criticism, agreed that the prose "overshadows" the verse, and varied Woodberry's "imperfect faculty of expression" only verbally, saying that the technical weaknesses of the poems spring not from "want of pains" but from "want of capacity in the artist." But then, with some disregard for consistency, the writer adds that the poems are still just "as well worth attention" as the essays and that some of them at least "are more unified, having an organic wholeness," which the prose in general tends to lack.[43] Though all this may leave us perplexed, we have the impression that the writer has read the poems and thought about them freshly, an impression not at all given by the next two literary histories to appear. In 1911 Halleck's *History of American Literature* repeats the judgment that Emerson's "prose overshadows his poetry," and agrees that nevertheless "some of his verse is of a high degree of excellence" despite its many "limitations," which include its

---

[42] George Edward Woodberry, *Ralph Waldo Emerson*, New York, Macmillan, 1907, pp.158-177. The quotations are all from pp. 158 and 167.

[43] *A Manual of American Literature*, Theodore Stanton, ed., "In Collaboration with Members of the Faculty of Cornell University," New York, G. P. Putnam's Sons, 1909, pp. 290-294.

"halting lines" and lack of "warm human feeling."[44] Similarly, Cairns's *A History of American Literature* in the following year lists all the usual deficiencies of the verse and adds a new one ("The 'Threnody' shows too intense personal sorrow to compete with smoother and more academic elegies."), but concludes with the absolutely unchallengeable observation that "Despite all this technical criticism the poems have a wonderful charm for many readers."[45] Clearly, the lack of a consensus on the value of Emerson's verse during these years was driving conventional academic minds to their wits' end. Bronson's solution of the difficulty was essentially the same as Cairns's: he first lists, as a matter of common agreement, all of Emerson's faults as a poet, with particular emphasis on his "deficiency of music," but then, not to seem unfair, admits that "occasionally, as in the *Concord Hymn*," Emerson wrote admirable poems. His concluding judgment bears so little relation to all that precedes it that we have to remind ourselves that Bronson was not a wit and intends neither humor nor ambiguity, simply "balance": "For sententiousness in verse Emerson has no equal among English-speaking poets of the nineteenth century."[46]

In 1915 O. W. Firkins devoted the chapter on "Emerson As Poet" in his critical biography chiefly to a thoughtful survey of the many reasons for the sharp differences of opinion on the subject. There was, he pointed out, increasing agreement on what were Emerson's strengths and weaknesses, but none on how high or low finally to rank him as a poet. "The passages which transport the believers are enjoyed by the skeptics; the faults which the assailants detest are pain-

[44] R. P. Halleck, *History of American Literature*, New York, American Book Co., 1911, pp. 188-191.
[45] W. B. Cairns, *A History of American Literature*, New York, Oxford University Press, p. 236.
[46] Walter C. Bronson, *A Short History of American Literature*, Revised and Enlarged Edition, Boston, D. C. Heath, 1919, p. 208.

ful to the defenders." Though there could be no question, he thought, about the "frequent and flagrant badness of Emerson's versification," and the "hopelessness" and the "obviousness" of his prosodic faults, the "main difficulties" in Emerson's poems were, if possible, even more serious: "want of organization . . . and want of imagination." Though Firkins's tone appears to be friendly and sympathetic, and though he predicts that opinion will continue indefinitely to be divided on whether to place Emerson as a poet among "the prophets shot with ineptitudes or the bunglers visited with inspirations," still the effect of his total discussion is to leave one wondering how any reader of taste can value poems that are bad as verse, poorly organized, and unimaginative. In Firkins's frequently cited and often praised book, it seems to me that criticism of the poetry reached an impasse.[47]

A few of those who wrote on our literary history in the next fifteen years or so seem to have wondered also how one could give a high rating to the poetry Firkins had described and decided that one couldn't, though the reasons for their low estimates are varied. Clement Wood in his *Poets of America* expressed the iconoclasm of the twenties when he decided that the best that could be said for Emerson's poetry was that he came closer to being a poet than his once-popular contemporaries, the Schoolroom poets. But American poetry, he felt, really begins with Poe, for in Emerson there is only "the scattered stuff of poetry."[48] A little later Russell Blankenship in his Tainean study, *American Literature as an Expression of the National Mind*, seems to have discovered no national characteristics in Emerson's poetry. We detect Blankenship's private reaction when he says that Emerson sounds "hopelessly old-fashioned" because of his

[47] O. W. Firkins, *Ralph Waldo Emerson*, Boston, Houghton Mifflin, 1915, pp. 274-296. The quotations may be found on pp. 274, 276, and 286.

[48] Clement Wood, *Poets of America*, New York, Dutton, 1925, pp. 9-11.

Transcendental ideas, but for the rest of what he has to say
he falls back on the standard list of "faults," condemning
the poetry as lacking both "verbal melody" and "sensuous
beauty," and the poet as lacking "sufficient command of
poetic technique." Despite the preoccupation announced
in his book's title, it does not occur to Blankenship to wonder about a possible connection between "the national
mind" and precisely these failures to satisfy traditional poetic expectations, particularly British Victorian expectations.
Still, the student reader is warned not to conclude that
Emerson's poems are "slight in value. On the contrary, they
are of high worth," though the author apparently cannot
think why. "High worth" or no, they are not good enough
to warrant any higher praise for Emerson than that he "was
probably the best poet of the Concord group."[49]

The treatment given the poetry by Parrington and Calverton about the same time is both easier to understand and
incomparably more intelligent. As liberal ideologues interested in literature chiefly as document, they could not be
expected to make much of the poems, but at least they did
not contradict themselves or fall back on conventional judgments irrelevant to their central theses. Parrington in his
Main Currents in American Thought does not treat the poetry except to quote part of "Politics" for its content, while
Calverton in *The Liberation of American Literature* rejects
it because it "never attained the Americanness" which he
believed our literature should express. Emerson's only importance, he asserts, lies in his influencing, and then recognizing, Whitman, "the first American poet." Since Calverton
finds that Emerson's "doctrines of self-reliance and self-
dependence" were "distinctly a product of the frontier,"
even though Emerson never saw the frontier until long
after he had developed the doctrine Calverton unaccountably divides into two doctrines, it seems odd that the author

[49] Russell Blankenship, *American Literature as an Expression of the
National Mind*, New York, Henry Holt, 1931, pp. 290-303.

could find no "Americanness" in the verse itself, even if only in its typical "faults."[50] Had he read the poems carefully before forming his judgment, we wonder.

Firkins's critical dead end had resulted from trying to weigh unquestioned "technical faults" against equally unquestioned "inspirations." But the "Poetic Renaissance," with its emphatic rejection of the conventions of British Victorian poetry, was already well under way when Firkins' book appeared, and during the years when Wood, Parrington, Blankenship, and Calverton were writing it had become the dominant force in poetry itself, even though many of the most eminent scholarly historians continued to write as though nothing had happened in poetry since Tennyson and Arnold. To the more perceptive critics, it gradually became apparent that Emerson's "faults" as a verse writer would have to be reconsidered. At the same time, the characteristic thought patterns of the twenties were increasingly hostile to Emerson's brand of idealism, as even Blankenship, never notable for his literary perceptiveness, had noticed. "Modernism" in verse and in thought had cast doubt, in short, on both of Firkins' certainties, that technically Emerson was a "bungler" and that prophetically he was truly inspired. It was time for someone with a renewed sense of the possibilities of poetry and of thought to start reading the verse again.

During the years between 1915 and the early thirties Emerson's poetry found six prepared and sympathetic readers whose judgments of it reflected their personal responses and ought still to command our attention. Paul Elmer More, Stuart Sherman, Alfred Kreymborg, Henry Seidel Canby, Bliss Perry, and Ludwig Lewisohn, who could hardly have been more different sorts of men in age, background, temperament, and outlook, wrote original and intelligent, and mainly favorable, discussions of the poetry that strike me

[50] V. F. Calverton, *The Liberation of American Literature*, New York, Scribner's, 1932, pp. 276-277.

as the only treatments worthy of their subject written during these years. Modern discussion of the subject begins with what these men wrote.

More had discussed "The Influence of Emerson" in his first collection of *Shelburne Essays* in 1906 but without treating the poetry as such. On the whole, he had thought at that time, the influence of "a faded and vulgarized transcendentalism" was a bad thing and Emerson had proved a mischief to weak minds. But with Emerson himself obviously so much more intelligent than his followers, More could even then count himself among "those . . . who are lovers of Emerson." Transcendentalism might be fading but "our sage of Concord" would persist. As it turned out, Emerson did not so much simply continue to be important to More as to grow in favor. More's chapter on Emerson in *The Cambridge History of American Literature* (1917) calls him "the outstanding figure in American letters," decides that his poetry at its best is far better than Arnold had said, and finds its general tendency toward "looseness and formless spontaneity of style" not inconsistent with the existence of occasional poems of great beauty. Though these triumphs are "rare" in Emerson's work, still, if they "had come oftener, he would have been . . . one of the very great poets of the world."[51] The poetry had never before received such high praise from so well qualified a critic.

Though More's praise is couched in aesthetic terms, it seems clear that, like Charles Ives, he took Emerson to be, in both his prose and his poetry, a spiritual voyager in uncharted waters. More's own spiritual odyssey would lead him eventually in the opposite direction from Emerson's,

[51] *Shelburne Essays*, I, New York, G. P. Putnam, 1904, pp. 71-84, and XI, Boston, Houghton Mifflin, 1921, pp. 69-94. The 1921 essay (vol. XI) is a reprinting of the chapter More had done for *The Cambridge History of American Literature*. For a discussion of More's changing attitudes toward Emerson, see Rene Wellek, "Irving Babbitt, Paul More, and Transcendentalism," in *Transcendentalism and Its Legacy*.

to Catholicism, but he found Emerson's poetic notes on the voyage always authentic and intelligent, and often moving. No doubt More's own debt to neo-Platonism prepared him to be sympathetic to Emerson, as the tinge of Marxism in Parrington's thought may have predisposed him to be unsympathetic.

In 1921 the then widely respected Stuart Sherman introduced his edition of *Essays and Poems of Emerson* with enthusiastic praise, with particular emphasis on Emerson's anticipation of "the poets of the present hour." In 1924 he expanded his remarks into the glowing tribute included in *Americans*. Emerson was, he thought, our liberator, a "true emancipator" who had freed us for fresh spiritual adventures. The "center of his being" was not ethical, as commonly held, but religious. "Religious emancipation as conducted by Emerson makes a man not less but more religious." His verse, which is often strikingly "modern," has offended readers by its unconventionalities, but it is time the critics stopped harping on its defects and saw it for what it is, strong wine. "He has been underrated as a poet because he did not understand, or would not practice, dilution."[52]

Alfred Kreymborg, himself one of the new poets of the "Renaissance," a writer of free verse, treated "the intoxicated Emerson" in his *A History of American Poetry: Our Singing Strength* (1929) as an inspired forerunner. In Emerson's verse he found not only "the first rebellion against British poetry" but real poetic mastery: "There is no poet among us whose drunken poems equal Emerson's." Some of his poems might better, he believed, be described as "ecstatic hymns." Later poets are greatly indebted to him: "He is in the blood of every American original," whether they recognize it or not. There is excitement, "fire," in his work, though "the passion belongs to the soul, rather than

[52] Stuart P. Sherman, "Introduction" to *Essays and Poems of Emerson*, New York, Harcourt, Brace, 1921; and "The Emersonian Liberation," in *Americans*, New York, Scribner's, 1924, pp. 63-121. The complete sentences quoted are from pp. 79 and 115 of the later work.

the body," which it remained for Whitman to discover. As for the always enumerated "technical faults" that so trouble grammarians, rhetoricians, and prosodists, they were, to be sure, "apparent on every other page" but finally unimportant in view of what the best poems accomplish. "Emerson was an artist and more. . . . What is a poet if he be not a man first of all?"[53] The earlier treatment that Kreymborg's passionately engaged and imaginatively penetrating discussion most suggests is that of Chapman, though the poet rates the verse higher than the essayist Chapman had.

In 1931 Canby devoted a chapter to Emerson in his *Classic Americans* and Bliss Perry published his still important *Emerson Today*. With less breadth and depth of learning and less catholicity of taste than More and less original minds than Kreymborg and Lewisohn, both men still managed to produce discussions of Emerson that have more than merely historical interest. Both writers decided that Emerson was, and is, more important than his accomplishment in his verse, even though both read the poems sympathetically and took them seriously. For Canby, Emerson is without question "the greatest intellect . . . in American history," the writer with "the most interesting mind," the true representative man of his time and place. Though he "may be a minor poet . . . he is a major prophet." The merits of his poetry are, in general, "prose merits," but he was capable of great lines and brief passages. Still, Canby concludes, "How tame his rather tiresome four-stress metres are beside the surging eloquence of his best prose! How feeble and limited his scope in verse" by the same comparison.[54] Perry's approach and conclusions are generally similar, though he seems at once to be more conventional and to be trying harder than Canby to do justice to the verse,

[53] Alfred Kreymborg, *A History of American Poetry: Our Singing Strength*, New York, Coward-McCann, 1929, pp. 67-83.

[54] Henry Seidel Canby, *Classic Americans*, New York, Harcourt, Brace, 1931, pp. 143-183, esp. pp. 169-171, on the demerits of the verse.

the "excellencies and defects . . . [of which] are so patent
that schoolmasters deal with them swiftly." Like Canby, he
is not only more enthusiastic about but more at home with
Emerson's thought than with his verse, so it is not really
surprising that in the end he gives the last words in his discussion to a "devil's advocate," who argues that most of the
fine things the poems say could just as well have been said
in prose; that brilliant fragments do not make a whole; that
the prosody is often "harsh" and sometimes even "gro-
tesque"; and that the "pontifical" tone is often distressing.[55]
Between them, Canby and Perry sum up conventional wisdom on Emerson's literary achievement and offer some
thoughtfully discriminating judgments of his verse, though
we miss in them the uninhibited personal response to the
poems that we find in Kreymborg, and both write as though
they were slightly embarrassed by a conflict between an
unexplained and perhaps unexplainable allegiance to Emerson and respect for received opinion of his verse. The
standards of the "schoolmasters" whose swift and easy
negative judgments Perry's tone tends to belittle are finally,
it would seem, the only ones these two ardent Emersonians
have to fall back on when judging the verse.

Not so with Ludwig Lewisohn, whose *Expression in
America* the next year opens with sentences from "The
Poet" used as an epigraph on the title page: "All men live
by truth and stand in need of expression. . . . The man is
only half himself, the other half is his expression." Lewisohn
finds Emerson a "classic" writer, in his verse as well as in his
prose. That his verse is uneven in quality Lewisohn finds
not to the point, for the test of a classic writer is simply that

[55] Bliss Perry, *Emerson Today*, Princeton, Princeton University Press,
1931, pp. 59-97, esp. pp. 81-93. A dozen years earlier, in *The American
Spirit in Literature*, New Haven, Yale University Press, 1918, pp. 128-
129, Perry had stated as his own the opinions assigned in the later book
to the "devil's advocate," though even then he had found "here and
there" in the verse a "miracle" of "true beauty."

he has left "certain works or even pages" that "the youth of
each generation" finds important enough to reinterpret in
its own terms and thus to find in it what it needs.[56]

Like Kreymborg, Lewisohn, himself a creative writer and
expressionist critic rather than a "scholar" in terms ap-
proved by the scholarly Establishment of the time, writes
about the poems as though the "schoolmasters" had never
written about them, as though the cul-de-sac implicit in
Firkins' treatment had never existed. The author of some
nine works of fiction and one play, in addition to studies of
modern German literature and modern French poetry,
Lewisohn responded personally to Emerson's poetry and
felt quite capable of judging it in his own terms. Despite its
unevenness, he found the best poems very great indeed, at
least as great, he thought, as those written by any of our
poets. Seldom since friends like Sanborn had written about
it had Emerson's verse received praise like this. To be sure,
he found much "dross" in the verse, but *his* dross included
the "mystical element" that Chapman had pointed to and
that most earlier readers had valued as somehow redeem-
ing the verse from its faults:

> Turning to the poems we are back with the more familiar
> Emerson, with his gold and his dross. By dross I do not
> mean the defective measures, the gritty rimes, the sediments
> of a blank and conventional diction in the earlier poems.
> In the mass of his better work in verse these things are
> wholly negligible. The dross in the verse as in the prose
> is the vague mysticism, the feebly stubborn optimism, the
> frequent lack of even intellectual edge and fire. But when
> all this dross is simply neglected and put out of mind there
> remains a small body of verse not yet perhaps quite
> equalled by any formal poet in America.

No doubt Lewisohn's assumption about what literature is
and what its value for us consists in made it easier for him

---

[56] *Expression in America*, p. 136. The remaining quotations are from
pp. 132, 135, and ix.

to reach this conclusion. He states his assumption in his Introduction in a way that seems to claim more novelty for it than it has. Emerson would have put it a little differently but would have agreed, as would Whitman. Today, Lewisohn writes, we have a new type of reader, who looks to literature for "a road to salvation, the bread of life." The "bread of life" that Lewisohn, the self-described Freudian, found in the best of Emerson's poems was obviously not the bread found by the poetry's earlier admirers, but the very difference in what the poems were valued for points up the similarity in the responses: both the early admirers and Lewisohn read the poetry as memorable vatic utterance, as *Dichtung*.

Yvor Winters a few years later was reading the poetry in the same way, though he reached the opposite conclusion about its value. Attacking Emerson the man and all his works with scarcely controlled violence, he paid the poetry the compliment of taking it as seriously as Emerson himself could have wished. But the rationalistic, even doctrinaire quality of his objections to the values and views he found in the poetry reminds us, too, of the hostile reactions of the early religious reviewers who had detected and denounced Emerson's attacks on orthodoxy. For Winters as much as for Orestes Brownson, Emerson was simply a dangerous heretic and that was really all that needed to be said. It wasn't, though, all Winters did say. In a way that was more Emersonian than he may have realized, he concluded that bad art and bad doctrines equally could only proceed from a bad man. Emerson, he asserted, "at the core is a fraud and a sentimentalist, and his fraudulence impinges at least lightly on everything he wrote. . . ." The only reason Winters gives us for considering Emerson the man a "fraud" is that though he recommended mysticism, "he had no mystical life to give." Unlike Jones Very, whose verse Winters liked and promoted, Emerson, he thought, simply "never experienced that which he recommended."

But the character assassination in which Winters in-

dulged might have been subtracted without requiring any
change in his ultimate judgment. For Winters the finally
important thing was that Emerson's ideas were simply
wrong. With different ideas he might have been a good
poet, Winters admits, for, reversing the conventional nineteenth-century opinion, Winters believes that Emerson
"was by natural talent a poet of a good deal of power."
Even as it was, crippled by his false philosophy, he remained "by accident and on certain occasions a moral poet,"
as several of his most traditional poems illustrate. (Not "by
accident," Winters' preferences among poems are the same
as those of Emerson's most conventional late-Victorian
readers.) Still, despite a few accidental achievements in
verse, the crucial fact about Emerson for Winters is that,
as he says quite truly, "Emerson was the most influential
preacher to appear in America after Edwards." Unfortunately for later Americans, Winters thought, the content of
Emerson's preaching was not just vacuous but pernicious,
as Hart Crane's suicide seemed so aptly to illustrate.[57]

Winters' attack, the most severe Emerson's life and work
had ever been subjected to, was and remains important, for
it was an original, intelligent, and authentic reaction result-
ing in coherent judgments. Unlike so many of our academic
literary historians, Winters was neither confused nor overly
cautious, and he did not suppose, as many of Emerson's
early critics seemed to, that form and content are wholly
independent of each other and thus capable of being
judged separately. Like Emerson himself, he believed that
it is not meter but meter-making argument that controls any
poem good enough to be taken seriously. With D. H. Law-

[57] Yvor Winters, "Jones Very and R. W. Emerson: Aspects of New
England Mysticism," in *Maule's Curse: Seven Studies in the History of
American Obscurantism*, Norfolk, Conn., New Directions, 1938, pp. 125-
146. The quotations are from pp. 142-143 and 131. Winters blames Hart
Crane's suicide on Emerson in a later essay, "The Significance of *The
Bridge* by Hart Crane, or What Are We to Think of Professor X?" *In
Defense of Reason*, New York, William Morrow, 1947, pp. 577-603.

rence, as well of course as with Emerson and many others, he believed passionately that "The essential function of art is moral."[58] This being so, poetry that preached a bad morality could not be good poetry. He thought there were grave dangers in Emerson's Dionysian position—as I am sure there are. To be in a state of ecstasy is to be "beside oneself," out of control. But I would suppose there are dangers in any position, including the contrasting Apollonian one of Winters, including also the "position" of refusing to take a position. Be that as it may, Winters' critical attacks on Emerson demand to be taken seriously, for in Winters Emerson found a worthy opponent. It is not clear to me that the same could be said of any other detractor in our century.

Unfortunately, from the point of view of those who believe that in recent decades Emerson has been seldom understood or justly valued, Winters' condemnation almost certainly had more influence on Emerson's poetic reputation in the succeeding decades than Lewisohn's enthusiastic praise did. Though few later commentators have followed Winters in his moralistic stance, the force of his intelligence made it necessary to reckon with his views, and many who could not follow the reasoning that led to his judgments accepted the judgments themselves and found other reasons for them, usually aesthetic reasons supplied by the New Critical Poetics that dominated the campuses during the forties, fifties, and early sixties. The chief New Critics themselves (Winters was not a typical "New Critic," despite his inclusion in Ransom's book that gave the movement its name)[59] were silent on Emerson: he was not grist for their mill, his poems did not yield to their methods. But many of their followers would reach judgments as negative as Winters' while giving as their reasons, not that false ideas and dangerous morality resulted in poems that offend our sense

[58] *Studies in Classic American Literature*, p. 171 (Viking edition).
[59] John Crowe Ransom, *The New Criticism*, Norfolk, Conn., New Directions, 1941.

of truth and reality but that his poems fail because they lack verbal intricacy, intentional ambiguity, density of symbolic allusiveness, complexity, and, most especially, rhetorical irony.

And of course for the most part, with a few exceptions like the word-play in "Hamatreya," they do tend to lack these qualities, a fact which no doubt helps to explain why hardly any important critic since Lewisohn, and no critic young enough to have been deeply influenced by the New Criticism, has had much good to say for them. Scholars have studied Emerson's ideas, his sources, his prosody, and his aesthetic theories, and explications of several of his poems have multiplied, but, with the exception of Robert E. Spiller's favorable treatment in *The Literary History of the United States*, the opinions of the two most influential scholar-critics who have written about him in recent decades, F. O. Matthiessen and Stephen Whicher, have seldom been challenged. Matthiessen thought only "Days" a successful poem[60] and Whicher regretted that for the most part the poetry simply could not be judged to be good poetry in terms of the only critical standards he respected—even though, as he clearly implies, he sometimes found himself

[60] *American Renaissance*, New York, Oxford, 1941, "Book One," *passim*, esp. p. 55. It is interesting to note how close Matthiessen is to Arnold's position on Emerson as poet, despite all the differences between the two men. Like Arnold, Matthiessen holds Emerson the man, and his prose, in high respect; indeed, Emerson's organic theory of art becomes a touchstone for Matthiessen's whole book. But he still comes very close to a blanket condemnation of the verse, implying clearly enough what Arnold had stated, that Emerson was not a "legitimate" poet. He does this by citing with obvious approval Eliot's dictum that whereas prose may be "legitimately occupied with ideals," verse "can only deal with actuality" (p. 55). Since "actuality" for Matthiessen as for the early Eliot is shot through with irony, frustration, and the possibility of failure, it is hardly surprising that Matthiessen chooses "Days" as Emerson's only passably good poem, for "Days" records the speaker's failure to choose ideally among the gifts proffered by the veiled, enigmatic days. The poem, in short, emphasizes the same gap between "ideals" and "actuality" that is implied by Eliot's statement.

responding to certain poems positively. Whicher was closer to the position of John Burroughs and other early admirers than he realized. Sufficiently drawn to Emerson the man and his work to spend years studying and writing about him, he was yet compelled to admit that he could think of no way to defend the poetry against the charges of aesthetic failure necessitated by the critical norms of his time.[61] In

[61] Stephen E. Whicher, ed., *Emerson: An Organic Anthology*, Boston, Houghton Mifflin, 1957, pp. 407-411. Whicher begins his discussion of the poetry by admitting that, measured by a high critical standard, "the plain fact is that . . . Emerson was seldom a very good poet." After naming some of his rare successes and describing his poetic ideal, Whicher rehearses "the indictment of Emerson as a symbolist," finding it justified in terms of the best available critical theory. Yet he is not happy with this conclusion. Critical standards change, he knew, and "Emerson is a dangerous man to pigeon-hole." Surely there ought to be a place in poetry for "loose improvisation on a . . . theme." Certain passages in the poems "reach an incandescence not quite like anything else in literature. . . . The poet who could strike these notes will survive all criticism."

Whicher's dilemma was a real one. With critical orthodoxy seeming to require condemnation of Emerson's typical practice and with the scholarly studies up to his time concentrated chiefly on matters other than critical evaluation, there was quite literally no set of critical terms available to Whicher for defending Emerson's typically "loose" poems. The Emerson scholars were not so much answering the New Critics as ignoring them.

Not all the scholarly and critical studies were quite as irrelevant to his purposes, however, as Whicher seems to have assumed. Gay Wilson Allen's *American Prosody* (New York, American Book Co., 1935) had suggested that it would be better to talk about stresses in Emerson's verse than about conventional prosodic feet, though it is true that Allen then proceeded to describe Emerson's prosody in conventional terms. In 1946 the poet-critic Mark Van Doren, introducing *The Portable Emerson* (New York, Viking Press, p. 13), had found the poetry markedly uneven in quality but had concluded that "the best of him belongs with the best American poetry." Robert E. Spiller had treated the poetry with sympathy and given it high praise in his chapter on Emerson in *The Literary History of the United States* (1948) and again in his *The Cycle of American Literature* (New York, Macmillan, 1955). In 1950 R. L. Cook had reemphasized the peculiarly American quality of the poetry in his Rinehart Edition of *Selections*. In 1951 A. H.

the years that have passed since Whicher's somewhat embarrassed and heavily qualified defense in 1957, the poetry
has been so thoroughly out of fashion that attempts to arrive at a critical evaluation of it, or even to take it seriously
enough in critical terms to attempt to describe its features
and place it in our poetic development, have become rare

Quinn had found a link between Emerson's versification and Old
English practice, concluding that "One of the least valid of the
critical judgments of Emerson's poetry lies in the supposed roughness of its metre" (Quinn, et al., *The Literature of the American
People*, New York, Appleton-Century, 1951, Part II, p. 285). In 1953
F. I. Carpenter, whose 1930 *Emerson and Asia* (Cambridge, Harvard
University Press) had broken fresh ground, summed up existing critical
and scholarly opinion and knowledge in his excellent and still useful
Emerson Handbook (New York, Hendricks House, 1953), finding it
possible to defend a good many of the poems in traditional critical
terms. (In order to do so, he had to write as though the New Critics
had made no significant contribution at all to our understanding of
literature, as, in my opinion, they most certainly had.)

In the years between Whicher's anthology and the present, no consensus seems to have developed. R. H. Pearce's *The Continuity of
American Poetry* (Princeton, Princeton University Press, 1961), devoted
chiefly to a discussion of the ideas in the poetry, appears to imply a
low critical evaluation of the poems as reflecting rather than transcending the divisions of sensibility of the poet and his culture. In 1964
Jonathan Bishop defended the poetry of Emerson's prose, but only at
the cost of remaking Emerson in the image of a contemporary human-
ist (*Emerson on the Soul*, Cambridge, Harvard University Press). In
the same year Walter Blair discussed Emerson and Thoreau as poetic
"rebels against nineteenth-century forms," suggesting that the later
development of "free verse" is useful for a consideration of Emerson's
prosodic practices and asserting that he and Thoreau "found their
chief models in a seventeenth century school of unorthodox versifiers."
(Blair, Hornberger, and Stewart, *American Literature, A Brief History*,
Chicago, Scott, Foresman, 1964.) Also in the same year Josephine Miles
treated Emerson as a poet briefly but respectfully as a "figurist" in her
"Minnesota Pamphlet," *Emerson*.

But probably Walter Sutton came closer to expressing majority opinion when he spoke of the "mechanical rhythm" and "monotony" of the
verses and concluded that Emerson was only rarely "able to realize his
own precepts" in verse. "It apparently never occurred to Emerson that

almost to the vanishing point.[62] The reason for this dramatic decline of interest is not hard to understand: the paradigm or model of "good poetry" which has guided the thinking and the work of scholars and critics alike has very inadequate room for, and provides no really appropriate way of dealing with, the kind of poetry Emerson chiefly wrote.

---

his own ideal"—his organic theory as expressed most fully in the essay "The Poet"—"was more fully realized in the essay, which was, after all, *his* most congenial form." (*American Poetry*, Irvin Ehrenpreis, ed., New York, St. Martin's Press, 1965, p. 177.) In the same year the third edition of James D. Hart's *Oxford Companion to American Literature* gave three columns to Emerson but only two brief sentences to the poetry. The impression left by Hart that the poetry is hardly worth discussing was reinforced a year later by *Transcendentalism and Its Legacy*, in which none of the ten essays treats Emerson's poetry.

Three earlier scholarly articles on the poetry that Whicher must have known had made real contributions without, except partially in the last one mentioned below, addressing themselves directly to the heart of Whicher's problem. Frank T. Thompson's "Emerson's Theory and Practice of Poetry" (*PMLA*, 43, 1928, 1170-1184) called attention to evidences of the importance of both Coleridge and Wordsworth to Emerson. Nelson F. Adkins' "Emerson and the Bardic Tradition" (*PMLA*, 63, 1948, 662-677) showed that Emerson admired the poets (real and legendary) he considered "Bardic" long before he knew much about them except at second hand. In "Emerson's Rhymes" (*American Literature*, 20, 1948, 31-42), Kathryn Anderson McEuen answered the late Victorian charge that Emerson was incapable of rhyming correctly, pointing out that his practices anticipated those of contemporary poets such as Ransom, MacLeish, Aiken, and Auden.

[62] Evidence for this generalization may be found in the two officially sponsored review-summaries of scholarship and criticism on American writers that appeared in 1972. Floyd Stovall, reviewing Emerson studies in recent decades in *Eight American Authors: A Review of Research and Criticism* (James Woodress, ed., New York, Norton, 1972; sponsored by the American Literature Section of the Modern Language Association), organizes his unwieldy mass of material under some ten headings ("Public Affairs," "Science," "Philosophy," etc.) but finds no need to provide a separate category for critical discussions of the poetry since there are so few of them. In a category called "General Estimates" Frost's 1958 opinion that Emerson was "one of the four greatest Ameri-

In short, the history of Emerson's reputation as a poet contains a number of oddities. Though his poems have always had their admirers, except for a few years in the twenties and thirties the admirers have generally seemed unable or unwilling to express the reasons for their admiration in "literary" terms. By contrast, the detractors have usually offered specifically "literary," even "technical," reasons for what they have considered the weakness of the poetry. Though there has been some movement toward consensus on which are the best poems, the only judgment on which there has been anything approaching critical unanimity is that the verse is, to an unusual degree, uneven. Attempting to balance specific faults against vague virtues and to mediate judiciously between widely differing general evalua-

---

cans" is mentioned but the reason Frost gave, that Emerson is "the" American poet as Washington is "the" warrior and statesman is omitted. My own 1968 study of American poetry is also mentioned, but its acknowledged thesis is unaccountably changed from Emerson's centrality in American poetry to his centrality in "American literary history." Both instances have the effect of implicitly denying, by ignoring, Emerson's status as a *poet*.

John C. Broderick, reviewing scholarly work on "Emerson, Thoreau, and Transcendentalism" (J. Albert Robbins, ed., *American Literary Scholarship: An Annual: 1970*, Durham, Duke University Press, 1972; similarly sponsored by the same scholarly organization) acknowledges the state of affairs illustrated by *Eight American Authors* (Emerson's poetry is characterized as having been "out of fashion") but predicts a "renewed interest in the poetry of the Transcendentalists." Significantly, however, the only evidence he offers for this opinion, as regards Emerson's poetry, consists of my own book (*American Poets from the Puritans to the Present*, Boston, Houghton Mifflin, 1968; Dell paperback reprint, 1970), an article by Carl Strauch ("The Mind's Voice: Emerson's Poetic Styles," *Emerson Society Quarterly*, 60, 1970, 43-59), and an article he judges not worth even the briefest of summaries. Broderick's prediction, though I strongly suspect that time will prove its correctness, appears, from the paucity of evidence cited, to rest chiefly on intuition. The only further pieces of evidence I am aware of, the articles by Bloom and Yoder referred to in my first chapter, appeared too late to be noted by Broderick.

tions, literary historians have often seemed uncertain and even embarrassed when writing of the verse, not infrequently betraying their embarrassment by overt incoherence.

By and large, the admirers of the poetry give the impression of having been moved by it, even if they cannot tell us why, while the detractors—with Arnold and Winters as perhaps the most conspicuous exceptions—very often write as though the merest glance would enable any intelligent reader, and has been sufficient for them, to tick off its faults and weaknesses. It seems to me clear that the feelings and imagination, the psychological needs and drives, the personal value structures and belief systems of the admirers have, in general, been more directly involved by the verse than have those of the detractors, who, again with some exceptions, give the impression of having arrived at their judgments without reading and listening nonjudgmentally and responding personally before judging impersonally. One evidence of this would be the common note running through the praise of the most ardent admirers in both centuries: equally by Tyndall and Kreymborg, Burroughs and Lewisohn, the poetry is valued for pointing beyond itself toward something that can save us, the verities, the saving wisdom, the bread of life. The detractors, on the other hand, have also in both centuries, however different their critical standards, sounded a common note: they have found the poems deficient as "compositions."

In the chapters that make up the body of this book, I shall argue as persuasively as I can for three ideas: first, that it is more rewarding to approach Emerson's poems as unforgettably expressed illuminations than as "compositions"; second, that though much of the verse is indeed deficient as composition, the best of it is not; and third, that perhaps partly because Emerson never fully mastered a wholly appropriate style in verse—"mastered" in the sense that Whitman, Frost, and Pound, for example, mastered styles suitable for the expression of their sensibility even in poems and passages that strike us as "uninspired"—much of his best "poetry" is to be found in his prose, in which he was a master stylist, though not an experimental one.

This three-fold argument accepts, in essence, the reservations of Henry James and Chapman and comes close, I expect, to reexpressing the positions of More, Kreymborg, and Lewisohn.

CHAPTER I

Rediscovering the "Voyager of Light and Noon"

Emerson has long been a problem for modern readers. Should we read him at all? If so, why? What does he have to offer, what values capable of touching our lives may we expect to find in his work? And *how* should we read him, if we do? As a man of wisdom, "the Sage of Concord" his later contemporaries honored? As a gifted visionary, a "Seer," as William James reverently suggested? As "the" "Philosopher of Democracy," as John Dewey thought he deserved to be called? As "a Puritan mystic with a poetic fancy and a gift for observation and epigram," as Santayana called him? As Robert Frost thought of him, as "the" American poet, one of the four greatest Americans, the peer in poetry of Washington in war and statecraft, of Jefferson in political thinking, and of Lincoln in saving his country?[1] Or should it be as Emerson himself probably would have preferred and thought most just, as a "voyager of light and noon" like his beloved humble-bee, that "lover of the sun" and "Sailor of the atmosphere" who could be "Wiser far than human seer" and an inspiration to poets just because he trusted to instinct to guide his zigzag course toward the source of light?—as a sort of unfrocked priest or lay preacher, in short?

If I did not think that we should read him, read him with an open mind and heart as he has seldom been read for a long time now, and that we shall find unexpected rewards if we do so, I would not be writing this book. I shall try to suggest some of the rewards I think we may expect to find.

[1] The tributes of Santayana, James, Dewey, and Frost are probably most conveniently available in Konvitz and Whicher, ed., *Emerson, A Collection of Critical Essays*, Englewood Cliffs, New Jersey, Prentice-Hall, 1962.

But the more urgent problem is *how* to read him. Very serious objections may be raised against each of the ways just suggested. Santayana and Frost seem to me to offer us our best clues, but it is very far from self-evident that either man's way of describing Emerson is wholly just. Over and over again for more than a century thoughtful critics have found Emerson in no significant sense either a Puritan or a mystic and in no praiseworthy sense a poet. So too with the other labels. Each of them both can be and often has been denied or shown to be inappropriate.

For us in the waning years of the twentieth century perhaps none seems less likely to appeal as the appropriate, or even as a possible, way to read him than the one I put last —as a sort of priest of the sun—suggesting it might be the way Emerson himself would choose to be read. Yet since to close our ears to whatever news he has to bring us about light and noon is in effect also to deny that he can have value for us as sage, seer, philosopher, mystic, or poet—for we have denied him his essential *subject*—I want to consider this most fundamental denial first. For if he was wise, there must be some wisdom in what he has to say about the many and the One, the individual soul and the World-Soul, the perishing moments of time and the everlasting now. If he was a seer, there must be something real about the light he thought he saw shining on us "from within or from behind." If he was a philosopher worth reading, it must be possible to be a "philosopher" while having only a slight interest in the classic problems of philosophy and despising logic and rigorously systematic thought. If he was a "Puritan mystic," it must be possible to say something valid about the light and noon waiting to be experienced from the proper vantage point without the benefit either of Puritan theology or a well-worked-out formulation of the nature and the means of attaining mystical experience. If he was a significant or even great poet, as not only Frost but Robinson and other poets have thought, it must be, as Frost said, as a "philosophical poet." But a philosophical poet whose technical virtuosity has never impressed even his contemporaries and whose "philosophy" strikes us as not just technically inexpert but truly vacuous is not likely to seem worth reading.

It is not, for most potential readers at least, because we think we know better answers to the problems he faced than those he found that we tend to doubt that he is worth reading, or reading again. We are much more likely to have decided that there are no answers to find, so that any he thought he found are proof of his naiveté. We have been taught by Existentialists from Nietzsche to Sartre that we must "create" the meanings once given us by the faith, must, if we are to reject despair, impose a meaning, a Supreme Fiction, on what may, for all we can know, have no meaning. The only escapes from the terror of history, we are likely now to think, lie in either disengagement or a willed affirmation of the truth of what we know cannot be tested. But insofar as we recognize those meanings we commit ourselves to as "imposed," not "discovered," just to that extent they fail us when we need them.

I suspect it may be an illusion that we are the first to find ourselves having to create a faith because the received one has failed us. Emerson, like many another poet and many another man, found the spur to all his thinking, to the chartless voyage of his imagination, in his conviction of the utter failure of the received faith. Assuming that we owe it to ourselves to reject despair, we ought to find his voyages toward light and noon speaking to our concerns, so far as the reports he brought back seem to us discoveries, not the impositions of will or the creations of fantasy.

Listen to Martin Heidegger writing in "What are Poets For?" of one of his own favorite poets, Hölderlin:

" . . . and what are poets for in a destitute time?" asks Hölderlin's elegy "Bread and Wine." We hardly understand the question today. How, then, shall we grasp the answer that Hölderlin gives?
" . . . and what are poets for in a destitute time?" The

word "time" here means the era to which we ourselves still belong. For Hölderlin's historical experience, the appearance and sacrificial death of Christ mark the beginning of the end of the day of the gods. Night is falling. Ever since the "united three"—Herakles, Dionysos, and Christ—have left the world, the evening of the world's age has been declining toward its night. The world's night is spreading its darkness. The era is defined by the god's failure to arrive, by the "default of God." But the default of God which Hölderlin experienced does not deny that the Christian relationship with God lives on in individuals and in the churches; still less does it assess this relationship negatively. The default of God means that no god any longer gathers men and things unto himself, visibly and unequivocally, and by such gathering disposes the world's history and man's sojourn in it. The default of God forebodes something even grimmer, however. Not only have the gods and the god fled, but the divine radiance has become extinguished in the world's history. The time of the world's night is the destitute time, because it becomes ever more destitute. It has already grown so destitute, it can no longer discern the default of God as a default.

Because of this default, there fails to appear for the world the ground that grounds it. The word for abyss—Abgrund —originally means the soil and ground toward which, because it is undermost, a thing tends downward. But in what follows we shall think of the Ab- as the complete absence of the ground. The ground is the soil in which to strike root and to stand. The age for which the ground fails to come, hangs in the abyss. Assuming that a turn still remains open for this destitute time at all, it can come some day only if the world turns about fundamentally—and that now means, unequivocally: if it turns away from the abyss. In the age of the world's night, the abyss of the world must be experienced and endured. But for this it is necessary that there be those who reach into the abyss.

The turning of the age does not take place by some new god, or the old one renewed, bursting into the world from ambush at some time or other. Where would he turn on his return if men had not first prepared an abode for him?

> How could there ever be for the god an abode fit for a
> god, if a divine radiance did not first begin to shine in
> everything that is?[2]

A little later in the same essay Heidegger might well
seem to be writing of Emerson rather than of Hölderlin:

> Poets are the mortals who, singing earnestly of the wine-
> god, sense the trace of the fugitive gods, stay on the god's
> tracks, and so trace for their kindred mortals the way to-
> ward the turning. . . . To be a poet in a destitute time
> means: to attend, singing, to the trace of the fugitive gods.
> This is why the poet in the time of the world's night utters
> the holy.[3]

To the extent that we recognize that we are living in the
dark and destitute time Heidegger posits, we ought to be
interested in reading Emerson's reports of his attempts to
learn to "see" the shining through of what, foreseeing mis-
interpretation, he usually scrupled to call "God" or the "divine," but was not embarrassed to describe as "the eternal
generator" of circles.[4] Living in a time and place too late for
the priests and too early for the psychiatrists, Emerson had
to make do with what was available to him, which was
chiefly the Blakean and Wordsworthian intuition that Nature, when seen in the right way, discloses ultimate meaning and purpose. His "natural supernaturalism" permitted
him to avoid at once the sterilities of both Stoicism and Aestheticism and the absurd bravado of supposing, with Hen-
ley, that he was the master of his fate and the captain of his
soul. It was, I think, chiefly because he continued to affirm
life's meaningfulness while avoiding all of the religiously
orthodox and most of the philosophically easy answers
available in his time that he seemed a sage to his contemporaries. For much too long now, for a generation at least, we
have assumed, without really rereading him attentively,

[2] Martin Heidegger, *Poetry, Language, Thought*, Albert Hofstadter,
trans. and ed., New York, Harper and Row, 1971, pp. 91-92.
[3] *Ibid.*, p. 94.   [4] In "Circles," in *Works*, II, p. 297.

that his answers were *all* too easy, his affirmations always
shallow. Noting the absence of rhetorical irony in his style,
we have concluded that his vision was defective because it
ignored life's ambiguities. If, reading him again, we can discover for ourselves that any part of the light he thought he
saw shining, paradoxically, through phenomena surrounded
by the darkness of time and death is really there to be discovered, not just invented, we shall be by that much the
gainers.

Still, it seems doubtful that Emerson will come again in the
foreseeable future to seem to be either a true "sage" or
"seer" in the senses intended by his nineteenth-century admirers when they used those words to praise him. It is all
too easy to "explain" what his age took to be his wisdom in
terms of the age's situation and needs. Listen to Alfred
Kazin, for example, describing Emerson's position, making
it in effect a foil for the superior "ghost sense" of Hawthorne. There is no need for Kazin to distort that position
to make it seem a little silly:

> Emerson, a remarkable writer of *pensées*, never believed
> in men or institutions so much as he believed in God as
> pure spirit, a god who dwells in us as our religious and
> moral imagination. Emerson believed—he allowed himself
> to believe—only in moral intuitions. Pure spirit was the
> greatest intuition, for that had become the moral law with-
> in us. Toward everything else on earth, Emerson could
> be smoothly ironic; so his marvelous journals became frag-
> ments of light, a wisdom literature that sometimes lost the
> light but never the appearance of being wise. This was
> what the Puritan tradition had left New England in the
> 1830s and 1840s, when American literature really began:
> a faith that literature could still be scripture. The writer
> was seen as an oracle, orator, and teacher who could give
> out the word that connected the people of God with God.
> Everything in nature manifested God's presence, and every
> word that the gifted prophet-poet could find in his heart

was a symbol of the divine truth. The Church was unnecessary, for God was everywhere, especially in the imagination
of Transcendentalists. There could be no anxiety or strain
as to the meaning of the creation, for all symbols found in
nature easily reflected God as clear and perfect truth.[5]

Or read Quentin Anderson's description of Emerson's
flight from society into the empire of self. It is not difficult,
Anderson explains persuasively, to understand why Emerson's audience, which "was not so much created by an artist
as found by a preacher," mistook his ideas for wisdom. He
reassured them by filling a vacuum in their failing belief
system, but, Anderson continues,

> How many [of Emerson's audience] understood that in the
> Emerson of the brave and desperate years—the 'thirties to
> the early 'forties—the guarantee of their connection with
> the universal was their existential uniqueness? No doubt
> many found in Emerson simply a fresh and rather titil-
> lating way to be good, to announce their ties to right feel-
> ing despite their having discarded a creed. But we have
> reason to believe that many of Emerson's hearers under-
> stood and welcomed the tie between themselves and the
> nature of things because it answered the same emotional
> need in them that it fulfilled in Emerson himself: the road
> to transcendence lay through self-absorption, one had to
> take possession of the imperium of one's own consciousness.[6]

I have not quoted these two explanations of why Emerson's contemporaries thought him wise in order to try to
show that the accounts are wrong. We may detect a slight
tone of amused superiority in Kazin's description of Emerson's position, and Anderson is openly hostile to Emerson's
antinomianism, finding in it, no doubt correctly, a threat to
an ordered society. But my point is that there is too much
truth in Kazin's description of Emerson's position and in
Anderson's remarks on his meanings to his admirers to

[5] "The Ghost Sense," *New York Review of Books*, 11:7 (October 24, 1968), 26.
[6] *The Imperial Self*, New York, Knopf, 1971, pp. 46-47.

make it seem likely that even the most sympathetic rereading will soon again persuade us to accept Emerson as a sage
or seer. And there is almost as little likelihood that we shall
come to think of him as a "philosopher," despite the moving
tributes to him by James, Santayana, and Dewey. For philosophy has come to be for us an academic discipline requiring neither the instinctive or intuitive wisdom of the
sage nor the visionary powers of the seer: clear, systematic
thinking about abstract problems, rather. Philosophy is
"done" in our time, not intuited, felt, or yielded to insight.
True, Morton White's recent history of American "philosophical thought from Jonathan Edwards to John Dewey,"
Science and Sentiment in America, rather surprisingly includes Emerson as a "philosopher," but, as it turns out, one
whose position was so far over on the side of "sentiment"
that White finds himself unable to think of any philosophic
contribution made by Emerson, and is forced to fall back
on paraphrase and quotation of the praise given him by
James, Santayana, and Dewey to justify his inclusion in the
book.[7] How indeed could a man who despised logic and
disdained to argue, except by the anti-rationalist method of
paradoxical assertion, contribute to the clarification, to
say nothing of the solution, of the classic problems of
philosophy?

Actually, since neither James nor Dewey had much respect
for metaphysical system builders and neither thought of
philosophy as primarily language analysis, they were not
praising Emerson as a "philosopher" in either of the two
senses the word is likely to have for us today but rather,
once again, as a sage or seer, a wise man. Santayana's praise
seems more to the point today. Significantly, he included it
in a book entitled not anything about philosophy but *Interpretations of Poetry and Religion.*

[7] *Science and Sentiment in America,* New York, Oxford, 1972, pp.
97-119.

Santayana concludes that Emerson, if not a star of the "first magnitude," is "certainly a fixed star in the firmament of philosophy" despite the fact that "at bottom he had no doctrine at all," he could not have defined any of his key terms, he never attempted to articulate his philosophy, and it does him an injustice to consider him as "primarily a philosopher." "The rare quality of his wisdom was due less to his reason than to his imagination. . . . Imagination, indeed, is his single theme." His importance to philosophy rests on the fact that, as Santayana sees it, philosophy must take serious account not only of science, which deals with fact, but of poetry and imagination also, which leave fact and clarity of understanding behind and are blended in religion. Actually, Santayana thinks, Emerson *had* no philosophy: "His was not a philosophy passing into a religion, but a religion expressing itself as a philosophy and veiled . . . in various tints of poetry and science."

It was Santayana's dualistic epistemology that allowed him, unsympathetic though he was to Puritanism, to mysticism, and to Transcendentalism, to accord to Emerson, despite his muddled thinking, a very high place in American philosophy. The same dualism allowed Santayana to be and remain both a scientific positivist and a Catholic. Few philosophers since have thought his position a tenable one, and there is no need for us to adopt it ourselves, even as a "working hypothesis," in order to recognize how clearly Santayana's concluding eulogistic statement of Emerson's importance points in the direction most likely to prove rewarding in any fresh rereading of Emerson today. "Alone as yet among Americans, he may be said to have won a place . . . [among the fixed stars "in the firmament of philosophy"], if not by the originality of his thought, at least by the originality and beauty of the expression he gave to thoughts that are old and imperishable."[8]

[8] "Emerson" in *Interpretations of Poetry and Religion*, New York, Scribner's, 1900, pp. 217-233 *passim*.

There is no conflict between these words of Santayana's published in 1900 and the tenor of Frost's 1959 speech "On Emerson," in which he named Emerson as his favorite poet and a great one even while making clear his dissent from Emerson's philosophy. "I have friends it bothers when I am accused of being Emersonian, that is, a cheerful Monist, for whom evil does not exist, or if it does exist, needn't last forever. . . . A melancholy dualism is the only soundness. The question is: is soundness of the essence." Santayana might have put Frost's final question a little differently: Is clarity of systematic speculative thought about matters of fact the only concern of philosophy? Like Santayana too, Frost defines Emerson as, alternatively, "a poetic philosopher" or "a philosophical poet." Santayana might have felt it a treason to his profession to add to this, as Frost did, "my favorite kind of both," but he too was a poet and spent the better part of his long life, after leaving Harvard in retirement, pondering imagination's mysterious role in life.[9]

Santayana and Frost, then, more than James or Dewey, seem to me to suggest the course the much-needed upward reassessment of Emerson should take. Whatever our own philosophic or religious position, it can hardly fail to seem to us that Emerson's true realms are the realms of "Poetry and Imagination," to borrow the title of his last great published essay. His "philosophy," so far as he may be said truly to have had one, is not likely to satisfy us, and as a religious reformer, he is generally much better as a critic of Christian—or perhaps any—orthodoxy than he is as a propounder of new doctrines. Though to be sure, if we don't take the word *doctrine* too literally, his religious insights often seem fresh and important. But after Auschwitz and Vietnam, who can believe in the inevitable operation of beneficent Progress, which Emerson called "the meliorative tendency" and treated as an article of faith—and which

[9] *The Idea of Christ in the Gospels* (New York, Scribner's, 1946) is perhaps the best evidence of this preoccupation of Santayana's in his later years.

Frost ridiculed in *A Masque of Reason*?[10] I at least find myself feeling only a little more sympathetic with his "philosophy" than Santayana did and no more so than Frost. Yet I find myself agreeing with them both about his seminal importance—I should say, with Frost, as a poet, which would seem to be what Santayana meant when he accorded him, as a man of imagination, a place of permanent importance in the firmament of philosophy.

But to propose that Emerson ought to be considered an important American poet is to be reminded immediately that his achievement as a poet has always, from the very beginning, been a matter of dispute. Many of the best literary critics in every period since his first volume of poems came out late in 1846 (dated 1847), beginning with Lowell, who thought he could not write "whole" poems, and Arnold, who reluctantly concluded that he was not a "legitimate" poet, have given him a very low rating or none at all as a poet. And, to make matters more difficult, the majority of the most ardent defenders have defended his poetry on what seem suspiciously like "non-literary" grounds. Unless one is prepared first to develop and articulate a whole new philosophical poetics created specifically for the purpose, how is one to defend Emerson as a poet not only against Lowell and Arnold and their followers but against all the "New Critics" and such luminaries as F. O. Matthiessen, not to mention the apparent majority of the most eminent scholars?

Only a fact not yet mentioned makes the attempt seem not totally hopeless if well enough done. It is that neither the "faults" alleged against Emerson as a poet by his critics in his own century and the earlier years of ours, nor the very different defects found in his work by the New

---

[10] The strange "tendency" referred to in the masque and described as a sort of magic carpet. See *The Poetry of Robert Frost*, Lathem, ed., New York, Holt, Rinehart, & Winston, 1969, p. 489.

Critics, on the one hand, nor the virtues found by his defenders, chiefly in the Pre-Modernist period, are likely to
satisfy us as unquestionably faults or unquestionably virtues—which would suggest that the whole matter of his
faults and his virtues needs fresh consideration.

The Victorian and post-Victorian consensus concerning
both the faults—faults so obvious that any schoolboy could
spot them, as one scholarly historian put it—and the virtues
were summed up with textbook concision in 1905 by the
author of a "manual" aimed at introducing high school students to American literature. The author opens his discussion of Emerson as a poet with these sentences:

> The question will ever be asked, "Was Emerson a great
> poet?" And just as often as the question is asked will an
> uncertain reply be given. It is not a difficult matter to de-
> tect flaws in his poetry; his rhythm is often faulty and at
> times his verse reads like prose, and yet he had a poet's
> soul. His prose is often poetry in disguise.[11]

As our survey of critical assessments of the poetry before
1920 has shown, the author here is simply reporting received opinion at the time. But by what standard, we wonder, is the rhythm of Emerson's poems being judged
"faulty," and just how "poetic" must a poem be to succeed?
As for the balancing praise, clearly it is not enough for a
poet to have a poetic "soul," and why, if he is a poet, should
he "disguise" his poetry?

Most of the New Critics seem to have found Emerson not
worth writing about as a poet, even to condemn, but
Matthiessen could not write his seminal book on the American Renaissance without treating Emerson and paying at
least some attenton to the poetry. Since he finds much to
admire in Emerson but does not admire the poetry, he
treats it very briefly and then chiefly to condemn it by referring to Eliot's dictum that though prose may legitimately
treat "ideals," poetry must deal with the ironic facts of life,

[11] James B. Smiley, *A Manual of American Literature*, p. 137.

as, all too obviously, Emerson's poetry doesn't. Matthiessen makes an exception of "Days," which he then proceeds to misread to deepen what he identifies as its irony.[12] But it is not at all clear that Eliot's notion of the proper spheres of prose and verse is of any use as a criterion by which to distinguish good from bad poetry. So once again, as we do when we read the earlier recitals of Emerson's "faults" as a poet, we feel that it is time to take a fresh look at what he wrote.

If the currently fashionable half-truth that the New Criticism is dead were taken at face value as the whole truth, it might seem surprising that the very negative evaluation of Emerson's poetry the New Criticism encouraged still lingers on unchanged in the graduate schools and the scholarly and critical journals, but such is the case, very clearly. Emerson's ideas, his sources, his relations to public events, and his aesthetic theories receive constant treatment, and minor obscurities of meaning in his poems are frequently explicated and reexplicated, but the nature and significance of his achievement as a poet must appear to most scholars to be questions too thoroughly settled too long ago to be of any interest today. Apart from my own earlier volume, only three writers, one a lifelong student of Emerson's poetry, have significantly broken the critical silence of recent years. Carl Strauch has defended the poetry as experimental and at its best highly effective in *The Emerson Society Quarterly*, Harold Bloom in two important essays has treated Emerson as a poet with great respect despite serious reservations about the Dionysian aspects of his thought, and R. A. Yoder has described Emerson's stylistic experimentation and his development of unique modes of expression in relation to his changing ideas of the poet in an impressive article in a recent issue of *PMLA*, "Toward the 'Titmouse Dimension': The Development of Emerson's Poetic Style."[13]

[12] *American Renaissance*, "Book One," *passim*, esp. pp. 55 and 59.
[13] Strauch, "The Mind's Voice: Emerson's Poetic Styles," *Emerson Society Quarterly*, 60, (1970) 43-59; Bloom, "The Central Man: Emerson, Whitman, Wallace Stevens" and "Bacchus and Merlin: The Dia-

Except for these four pieces, the failure of Emerson's poetry
to provoke critical discussion in recent years might seem to
make it proper to conclude that it is no longer necessary to
give an "uncertain reply" to the question "Was Emerson a
great poet?" The long debate might seem to be ended at
last, with the late-Victorian detractors and the Modernist-
New Critical theorists incongruously blending their voices
to say the last word.

The last word should properly be followed by silence.
But, perversely perhaps, I hope to break the silence, even
if only to suggest that both the Victorians and the New
Critics judged Emerson's verse by inappropriate paradigms, paradigms calculated to reveal its weaknesses—some
real and some imaginary—and obscure its characteristic
strength.

Emerson's aesthetic theories have been and continue to be
described, analyzed, and evaluated over and over again,
so often and so thoroughly that there seems little more that
needs to be said, or that even could be said without pointless repetition. Emerson believed that the poet must be inspired, breathed into by the Spirit, the World-Soul, which
would use him as its organ or mouthpiece, even dictating
his very words. The poet could achieve the prophetic status
proper to the true poet only by self-surrender, by learning
to listen with fully open ears and to see through (not "with")
transparent eyeballs, in effect by giving up his mere "understanding" and courting intoxication with the Transcendental wine of ultimate and unlimited Reality. His aesthetic
theories derived from Neo-Platonism, and both his theory
and a part of his practice of poetry were greatly influenced
by his understanding of the role of the primitive Bard and

lectic of Romantic Poetry in America," *The Ringers in the Tower*,
Chicago, The University of Chicago Press, 1971; and Yoder, *PMLA*,
87:2 (March, 1972), 255-270.

the characteristics of Bardic poetry. And so on. All this is too familiar to need further repetition.[14]

But I do want to try briefly to make just two points about Emerson's poetics. Most baldly put, they may well seem too obvious to need restatement. They are, first, that despite the large amount of truth in the idea that Emerson was neither consistent nor persistent in following out his theories in his practice, it is still true, as Adkins, Strauch, Yoder, and others have shown, that the theories he held help to explain both his triumphs and his failures; and second, that nothing that we have learned since his time, no "cumulative advance of knowledge" as it were, makes it necessary for us to discard his ideas about poetry and the poet as outmoded, mere relics of a literary movement long since past. Much of what I have to say about the first point, the relation between his theory and his practice, will be said later in the discussions of specific works and general traits of his work, and the idea I shall emphasize chiefly in this connection—because it seems to me never to have been adequately discussed—I shall delay until after I have said something about his poetic ideal. This seems then the proper time to say what I have to say about the second point, the "timelessness," as such things go, of his conception of poetry.

One may approach the subject by considering the meanings, including the etymology or history, of the words Emerson used or we must use to express his ideas. Emerson held to a "vatic" conception of poetry, we say, not always recalling that the Latin *vates* was not only a "diviner" but also a "prophetic speaker," in short a poet, without any distinction being insisted on between the divining and the speaking. Emerson defined the true poet, we recall, as the

14 My summary is not only "familiar" but oversimplified. Though it conveys the gist of "The Poet" and "Merlin" well enough, Emerson's ideas and practice changed with the years, though I think he never completely dropped, and certainly did not repudiate, important aspects of his Transcendentalism. See the Strauch and Yoder articles just cited.

"Namer" and "Sayer," words which, though not by linguistic derivation, repeat the meanings contained in the Latin verb *dicere*, to say, to speak. The German words for poet and poetry retain the meaning of the Indo-European root they share with the Latin word better than their English equivalents do. *Dichter* is defined as "Poet; writer (of fiction)," and *Dichtung* as "Poetry; poetical work; poem, fiction." To native speakers of German, I am told, *Dichtung* tends to connote condensed or otherwise memorable imaginative articulations of wisdom. In short, the ancient ideas that the poet is a man of imagination (as we should say) who may speak in either verse or prose, assuming that he speaks memorably and truly, and that his product, poetry, is similarly unrestricted as to its form, are better preserved in the German *Dichter* and *Dichtung* than in the English words. Emerson may not have known this, for his German was not good, but he would certainly have welcomed the knowledge, if he had had it.

The words Emerson was forced to use, "poet" and "poem," have a very different history, one not nearly so compatible with Emerson's ideas. "Poet" comes from a Greek word meaning "maker," "composer," which in turn is related to a Sanskrit word meaning "to pile up" and to an Old Slavic word meaning "to arrange." Etymologically, then, a "poet" is one who compiles, arranges, or composes *given* material. These are very different activities, it would seem, from saying or naming, which imply that what is to be said or named must first be divined, recognized, or seen for what it is. The definitions of "poet" and "poem" in *Webster's Third International* bear out our sense that the German and English words carry with them different emphases, particularly when we keep in mind the fact that the definitions start with the basic literal meanings and only then list the extended or figurative meanings:

Poet: "1. one who writes poetry: a maker of verses; 2. a writer having great imaginative and expressive gifts and possessing a special sensitivity to language; 3. a creative artist . . . whose work is marked by imagination. . . ."

Poem: "1. a composition in verse; 2. a piece of poetry designed as a unit and communicating to the reader the sense of a complete experience; 3. a composition, creation . . . likened to a poem."

Similarly, the first, and only literal, meaning given for "poem" in *The New English Dictionary* runs, " 'The work of a poet, a metrical composition' (Johnson); 'a work in verse' (Littre)."

In effect then when Emerson denied that a talent for metrical composition was sufficient evidence of being a poet, insisting rather that the true poet could be known only as his work proved him distinguished as a Namer and Sayer, he was, whether he knew it or not, and he almost certainly did not, returning to the root meanings of the German *Dichter* and the Latin *dicere*, found in the Indo-European *deik*, "to show, pronounce solemnly; also in derivatives referring to the directing of words or objects . . . betoken . . . say, tell"; and, at the same time, to the source of the Latin *vates*, the Indo-European *wāt*, "to inspire, spiritually arouse."[15] Neither a *Dichter* nor a *vates*, in short, was distinguished by a talent for a special kind of metrical composition in words so much as by the ability first to discern and then point to, pronounce solemnly as one with authority, give a token of, what existed waiting to be pointed to, named, or said. If the *Dichter* was also a *vates*, as Emerson thought he should be, his verbal pointing or pronouncing would "inspire" as it directed attention to the real. Since the *vates* was in touch with the gods, his words would be "artful thunder," as Emerson once most succinctly described the work of the true poet. For the achievement of such authoritative speaking, the fundamental conditions would be a special knowledge or awareness of what there

15 The Indo-European etymologies are from *The American Heritage Dictionary*, Appendix.

was that needed showing, pointing to, or pronouncing and the intention of making it known. Emerson's idea of the poet was not an invention, either of his own or of the British Romantics who preceded him, but a rediscovery of ancient meanings.

But of course not a "rediscovery" in the sense in which an archeologist excavating a buried city brings to light artifacts unaffected by time; a creative rediscovery rather. For Emerson's idea of the poet as truth-speaker blended the idea of the *bard*, the national poet who sings the history and exploits of his people, speaking both of and for them, with the idea of the *soothsayer*. The Indo-European root meaning of *bard* is "he who praises," while the archaic meaning of *sooth*, "truth, reality," derives from the word's Indo-European source in *es*, "to be," the source of Old English *eam*, "am," hence that which really *is* as contrasted with that which merely appears to be.

Combining the idea of praise attached to "bardic" with the idea of the true rather than the merely apparent *being* associated with soothsaying alters both ideas. As bard the poet will praise, but only that which really is, which perhaps only his special powers can divine; and as soothsayer he will be no Cassandra but will affirm and inspire, announcing and supporting a true faith more effectively than the priests, better even than the mystics. Insofar as the truths he wishes to state and praise are widely accepted by his people, the soothsaying bard can write gnomic, aphoristic verse. But if his truths are hidden from the understanding of his time, an aphoristic style will fail him.

Emerson's characteristic verse has often been described as gnomic, and up to a point the description is useful, but it seems to me to stop just short of pointing to an aspect of his style that is very prominent in much of his best, as well as in some of his poorest, work, and that makes it the kind of gnomic verse a bard might write if he felt that "his people" were few, that the mass of men were blind to the truths he was busy announcing and praising. I mean Emerson's very frequent reliance on paradox, in both his verse and his prose.

The tradition of paradox was ancient, it suited Emerson's purposes, and he was well acquainted with it as a way of writing. Paradoxes are statements, rational in their form, ordinarily made in the plain language of discourse, of apparent falsehoods which—if the writer succeeds with us—are found in some deeper sense to contain or point to truths. The learned Erasmus gave lavish praise to Folly, and Emerson, no fool himself, wrote that far and near are the same, and that "evil will bless and ice will burn." "Brahma" and "Uriel" are gnomic or vatic poems that succeed, if they do, because of the use they make of the literary tradition of paradox.

A number of the writers who are discussed in Rosalie Colie's definitive *Paradoxia Epidemica: The Renaissance Tradition of Paradox*,[16] were among Emerson's favorites, so it requires no speculation to discover how the tradition of paradox reached him and qualified his attempts at vatic poetry conceived, as he hoped, out of pure inspiration. As Colie puts it, the tradition of literary paradox practiced from the most ancient times, adapted to their purposes by Medieval writers in the tradition of "negative theology," and a favorite form of the Renaissance, was a very sophisticated literary convention, produced both by and for the cognoscenti, and a fragile one too, in a sense, since its success depended on its author's correctly judging the state of "received" or conventional opinion or belief relating to his subject, opinion or belief which he would then proceed to contradict. If he misjudged the popular mind, or if conventional opinion changed radically, his paradoxes would either seem pointless or be misinterpreted. A sufficiently radical change in the popular understanding of truth or propriety could even make his intended paradoxes come to seem to be "common sense."

[16] Rosalie L. Colie, *Paradoxia Epidemica: The Renaissance Tradition of Paradox*, Princeton, Princeton University Press, 1966.

Emerson to be sure was not self-consciously writing for
the cognoscenti—though in fact in writing for himself and
for the readers of *The Dial* he was in the early years doing
so—and he would no doubt have been displeased by being
told that he was drawing on not only a very ancient but
very "artificial" literary form. But the success of his paradoxes depended, and still depends as much as Cicero's or
Erasmus' ever did, on the existence of a conventional, widely shared set of opinions, attitudes, and values, which the
paradoxes deliberately upset or affront. That Emerson did
not often misjudge what would seem common sense to readers in his own time is shown by his reputation in that time
as a Sage (even though his poetry was considered "technically" or stylistically very "faulty"). But since "common
sense" differs somewhat from age to age, the successful paradox of one age may, as I have said, come to seem either a
pointless absurdity or a banal truism to another.

This seems to me to help to explain why some of Emerson's most ambitious poems fall so flat for many modern
readers. Particularly when he dealt with Nature, not in the
sense of the whole physical cosmos but in the sense of rural
landscape, Emerson's paradoxes have to a considerable extent lost their point for us. So long as the majority of Emerson's readers could be depended upon to identify Revelation with the Bible, it was shocking to find Emerson reading
Nature as Scripture. But if the idea of Revelation itself
comes to seem meaningless, what happens to the paradox?
Even "Hamatreya," surely one of the easiest of Emerson's
paradoxical poems for the modern reader to respond to,
and largely immune, unlike "Woodnotes," to the destructive
effect on its paradoxes of changed assumption about Revelation, has come to need some explaining. Its paradoxes
ridicule, make doubtful, what in the still predominantly
agrarian society of Emerson's youth seemed too obvious to
question, that is, that the degree of a man's wealth and power could be gauged by the amount of land he owned. In our
technological and corporate society, it is much harder for

us to get the point of the god's laughter at the "earth-proud" pretensions of the landlords. We are likely to come to the poem feeling that it does not require any god-like wisdom to see the absurdity of the attitudes attributed to the dead settlers. But who today would find it easy to laugh with the gods if a number of owners of large blocks of stock in giant conglomerates were to claim that their possession of the stock brought them real wealth and substantial power?

So Emerson often fails us as a poet even when we grant him the validity of his poetic ideal and his paradoxical way of achieving it, fails particularly in his verse, less often and less jarringly in the poetry of his prose. But he often succeeds, too, in both forms of expression, as I shall try to show. But his successes, particularly those in his verse, are more apparent when we approach them as important things impressively stated—solemn, often paradoxical, pronouncements—than when we approach them as aesthetic constructs, as things made, arranged, compiled, or composed. A handful of his very best poems, more of them than we may have thought, are well enough "made," to be sure, to count as distinguished poems by any standard, compositional or vatic, but even these seem more impressive when thought of as heightened memorable pronouncements than when examined as autonomous verbal artifacts or compositions.

Any poet we judge worthy of reading at all deserves to have his works read in the way that will best exhibit their virtue, their strength. The strength of Emerson's poetry lies in its imaginative articulation of perceptions of aspects of reality available only from his own special viewpoint, perceptions fresh at the time in the way he uttered them if not wholly without precedent, and—many of them at least—still capable of enlarging and refining our own perception of reality. Considered as intricately wrought verbal structures, most of his poems are unimpressive, and even the best of them may seem only moderately so. Considered as paradoxical, vatic, or gnomic utterances, his best poems exhibit the strength that so impressed Robinson, Frost, and other poets.

I said that my second point connected with Emerson's poetic theory was that we should think of it as "timeless" rather than as outmoded, and I have just suggested one reason why we should—that is, that if we do, we are more likely to be in a position to discover the special virtue of his poetry at its best; in effect, not to remain blind to whatever strength it has. But there is another reason too. In identifying the vatic and paradoxical elements in Emerson's theory and practice of poetry, I talked chiefly about their ancient lineage. But of course a theory or form may exist through many ages but then finally come to seem "outmoded."

The fact is, however, that an Emersonian poetics and certain aspects of his experimental practice, his style, have not only never become irrelevant to our later poets, as I showed in *American Poets, From the Puritans to the Present*, but are particularly in evidence today, as witness the belated recent "discovery" and recognition of that very Emersonian poet A. R. Ammons.[17] Far from being safely dead, buried in the textbook histories of literature, Emerson's idea of the poet as Namer and Sayer is very much alive.

[17] See A. R. Ammons, *Collected Poems, 1951-1971*, New York, W. W. Norton, 1972, and Harold Bloom's "A. R. Ammons: 'When You Consider the Radiance'" in *The Ringers in the Tower*. Bloom's article was the first serious critical study of Ammons' work.

CHAPTER II

The Apprentice Years: Composer of Verses

When he was still a small boy, perhaps when he was only nine, certainly by the age of ten, Emerson was impressing first his family and later his friends and teachers by the talent he showed for versifying. In an age when, in proportion to the population, more educated people than now read and wrote poetry, when poetry occupied a more prominent place in formal education, he still seemed distinguished by the apparent ease and obvious skill with which he could compose correct eloquent verses. Years later, writing of Shakespeare, "the" poet, in *Representative Men*, he would contrast poets with mere versifiers, remarking that though "Cultivated men often attain a good degree of skill in writing verses," such a talent does not entitle them to be called poets;[1] but in his school and college days he knew of course no such distinction. The verse of his maturity would often strike readers as rough and unskillful, and he himself once confessed that as a poet he spoke with a "husky" voice, but the chief impression to be gained from reading the verse of his school and college days preserved in *The Journals and Miscellaneous Notebooks* is one of the fluency and ease with which, from the tenderest years, he was able to express conventional ideas in conventional verse forms, at first those favored by the early eighteenth century, later those of the Pre-Romantics. His poetic juvenilia make it very clear that he had a high level of verbal facility and a good enough "ear" for verse forms to be able to imitate them flawlessly.

Boy and man, it would seem, when Emerson wanted to write conventionally smooth verse, and had the will and the

---

[1] *Works*, IV, p. 205.

time and energy to work at it, he could do so, as he did
equally in some of his earliest verse letters and in the mature "Concord Hymn." If at times his poetic voice really
was "husky," it was so principally when he let himself go
and wrote only to please himself, or when his mature poetic
theory made demands that could not be satisfied within the
conventions he had mastered and the skills he possessed. As
his ideas about the role of the poet and the function of poetry matured, he wavered between thinking the ability to
achieve smoothly polished verses one of the lesser gifts of
the poet and thinking that melodic verse was usually a mask
for inner emptiness. Late in life, after his productive years
were over, he seems to have moved back to a position closer
to that of his boyhood and youth than the one he had held
during his creative period. His valuation of Whitman's
verse went down, of Tennyson's up. "The Adirondacs," one
of his last major poetic efforts, is written in flawlessly conventional blank verse—by which I do not mean to belittle
the poem, for it remains an interesting, too little appreciated work, valuable for the quality of the mind we hear
speaking to us in a voice at once cultivated and colloquial,
an assured, easy, confident voice, equally at home with the
distinguished campers and the traditional verse-form.
When he prepared *Selected Poems* in the mid-seventies, he
excised from "Woodnotes II" the most irregular lines, at
once making the poem more acceptable to Victorian expectations and (from our point of view) greatly weakening it. By
1878 he may have come to agree with Arnold and Lowell
and the others who had found his verse faulty, at least if a
remark Sanborn says he made to him in that year reflected
a settled conviction and not a passing mood. "It has been
settled that I cannot write poetry," he said, declining Sanborn's request that he write a stanza to accompany a magazine article Sanborn was writing about him.[2]

Whether or not he could write good poetry as distinguished from competent verse, or had ever been able to, the

[2] Frank B. Sanborn, *Ralph Waldo Emerson*, p. 89.

evidence of the first decade of his versifying makes it clear that the traditionally smooth-flowing, accentual-syllabic verses he still sometimes produced in his maturity were not just happy accidents. Reading his earliest verse right through is likely to leave the impression that he might have rivalled Longfellow in smoothness if he had wanted to. If he ordinarily didn't, it was not for lack of an ear for the cadences of English sentences and conventional meters.

F. I. Carpenter went directly to the nub of the matter years ago in his remarkably durable *Emerson Handbook* when he opened his discussion of the verse with the statement, "First and last Emerson was a poet."[3] It is no accident that all of the earliest extant literary efforts are in verse. All through Boston Latin School, between the ages of ten and fourteen, and even more during his four years at Harvard (ages fourteen to eighteen) he thought of himself and was thought of by others as distinguished only in two ways, first because he was the late William Emerson's son and second because he had demonstrated unusual facility at versifying. At Harvard he was a mediocre student who often neglected his assignments, at that time still confined largely to the ancient languages and theology, in order to devote his time to reading English literature, which was not yet a part of the prescribed curriculum, and to versifying. His brother Edward was the "scholar" of the family, the brilliant one, as everybody knew. Waldo's only significant honor in college was being chosen class poet—by his classmates, not by the faculty.

He wrote serious verse to enter in competitions or to hand in as class exercises. He wrote humorous verses for his convivial Pythologian Society commemorating eating and wine-drinking feats and other escapades, the orgiastic nature of which he treated with understandable boyish exaggeration. He broke into verse frequently in letters to his

[3] P. 79.

brothers and friends, verse that still exists, unrevised, just as he wrote it down, and that quite often is almost as amusing as he hoped it would be. More significant, it seems to me, than the poetic ambition revealed in his polished serious efforts is just this fact, that he so often wrote verse simply for the fun of it, expecting it to be seen only by the recipient of the letter of which it was a part. Longfellow, in contrast, never, so far as we can tell from the letters and his biographers, wrote verse for anything but recognition, for the "eminence" he so singleheartedly pursued. Not that Emerson lacked ambition. Very unsure of himself as yet, and with good reason, considering his family's expectations and his undistinguished record as a student, he too longed to achieve "eminence" in some way, perhaps as an orator, perhaps as a poet—two avenues to power, both dependent on the skill with words everyone encouraged him to believe he had, that were often linked in his mind. Would he achieve eminence and power as a poet or as an orator? He wavered between the two and wrote a poem on "Eloquence." But he had a sense of humor and could smile even at his own ambitions, dropping into nonsense verse and transparently bad parodies at times to joke about the one talent he had thus far demonstrated, his somewhat precocious facility at versifying.

Both the abundance, variety, and frequent skill of the verse and the content of the statements about poetry in the letters and journals of Emerson's school and college years make it clear that the often-quoted sentence in a letter to Lidian before their marriage—"I am born a poet, of a low class without doubt yet a poet. . . ."—should be read as a sincere revelation of his self-image, despite the fact that both the context of the statement and the course of his later career might easily lead us to distrust it. As for the context, the statement is embedded in a letter the purpose of which is to explain to Lidian that if they are to be married, she must leave her beloved Plymouth home and move to rural Concord, because, as he goes on to explain, for a poet of the

"Correspondences" between the soul and matter, as he is, the natural rural beauties of Concord are very important to him, indeed essential if he is to go on being a poet. (Reading this, we are reminded of his request that Lydia change her name to Lidian, so that the excrescent "r" of New England pronunciation would not maker her "Lydiar Emerson" and thus him "Mr. Remerson.") Was his statement of his poetic vocation simply the most diplomatic way of informing his fiancée that if they were to live together, she would have to do the moving, not he, even though he had only recently settled in Concord and had as yet no real home there?

As for the later career, except for a brief period in 1845-1846, the greater part of Emerson's time and energies went into lecturing, corresponding, preparing his lectures for book publication as essays, attending to the duties of a father and a householder, and enjoying the role of gentleman farmer and orchardist on his ever-expanding Concord estate. He published just two slim volumes of new poetry during his lifetime. Only in the months when he was preparing his first volume for publication, filling it out with new poems, several of which turned out to be among his greatest, did the writing of poetry have the sort of first claim on his time and attention one gets the impression it had during his school and college years. If he really was, as he told Lidian, "born a poet," why was he so easily distracted from his real vocation? If the sense of vocation was really strong in him, why did he spend most of his time the rest of his life writing prose?

Yet despite such nagging doubts as these about how much weight we should attach to the famous statement of vocation, all the evidence from the school and college years suggests that however useful to him the statement might be as an argument in the question about who should move where, it still expressed his own sense of his potential sufficiently well to give him no reason to feel insincere in making it. (Even in the middle of it, of course, he had admitted that "My singing be sure is very 'husky,' & is for the most part in prose. Still am I a poet in the sense of a perceiver. . . .") The man who made the statement had either hoped to become or "professed" to being a poet all through his youth,[4] and he would later, as his ideas about the nature of poetry matured, move toward breaking down the accepted distinctions between poetry and prose. At the time when he made it, he was conceptually about midway between the schoolboy who could write his brother William that "But as even Nonsense sounds good if cloth'd in the dress of Poetry I believe I must resort to that as my last expedient"[5] and the mature author of "The Poet" who would argue later that it is not metre but metre-making argument that makes a poem and condemn Poe as a mere "jingle-man." Emerson's earliest verse and opinions about verse do little to prepare us for either the ideas about the poet and poetry for which he was later to become famous or the unconventional strength of the greatest poems he would later write, but they do persuade us of three things: that he thought his chief talent was for poetry rather than for philosophy, theology, or scholarship in the accepted senses; that he enjoyed versifying, even versifying "Nonsense"; and that he had a more than usual talent for versifying in perfectly conventional eighteenth-century forms. If he was not "born" a poet, he had at least practiced being one for many years before he announced his vocation to Lidian.

As I have already suggested, Emerson's school and college verses may be thought of as falling into two classes, the "serious" and the "light." The serious verse was written to

[4] For example, the statement in an 1816 letter to Edward, ". . . —but as I profess to be Poet I suppose you expect me to write 'Poetice' . . . ," whereupon the writer breaks into humorous heroic couplets. *The Letters of Ralph Waldo Emerson*, Ralph L. Rusk, ed., New York, Columbia University Press, 1939, I, p. 18.

[5] From another letter to Edward in the same year. (*Ibid.*, I, p. 25.)

be judged by his teachers, principally, or sometimes by a learned older friend and mentor. It was written to impress its readers with both his skill at versifying and his "scholarship"—for example, with his ability to translate Latin into fluent English verse. Required class "compositions" might be done in either prose or verse, and Emerson apparently sometimes chose verse as his medium, as in the lines headed "Beginning of Theme on Solitude," a fair copy of which may have been submitted in place of a prose composition. If so, the lines, with Emerson's later correction of a mental lapse by the deletion of the unneeded "d" and his smoothing out of the prosody by the deletion of the "ly" endings, probably pleased his junior year composition tutor, they were so perfectly what verse was expected to be at Harvard in 1820:

> To other worlds by roving fancy led
> The minstrel's airy pilgrimage was sp[d]ed
> There musing silent[ly] in majestic mood
> Abandoned by all things that lived he stood
> And pondered strange[ly] on Nature's low design
> Degrading man & all his powers divine,[6]

At other times the verse might be intended to be entered in a prize competition. In any case, it was a "public" form of verse reflecting the taste and expectations of educated Boston readers of the second decade of the century. The Romantic revolution ushered in by Wordsworth and Coleridge a few years before had not yet deeply affected the majority of Emerson's teachers and guides. Neoclassic forms were expected and the youthful poet was eager to please. Almost all of Emerson's surviving early verse that can clearly be identified as intended for public reading was written in couplets based on neoclassic models, either the "heroic" pentameter or the less "serious" tetrameter.[7]

[6] This and all subsequent quotations from Emerson's youthful poetry are, unless otherwise identified, taken from *JMN*, vols. I-II and VI; *Letters*, vol. I; and Rusk's *Life*.

[7] The chief departure from neoclassic couplets in Emerson's *serious* school and college verse came in the form of his occasional use of

The distinction between Emerson's serious academic or
public verse exercises and the light verse he wrote, chiefly
in letters to his brothers Edward and William just because
he enjoyed versifying, would be tidier if it could be said
that in these private or light verses he consistently used
other than neoclassic forms. The untidy truth is, however,
that in these verses too he generally used, or parodied, neoclassic forms, even for nonsense verse. But it is perhaps significant that it was *only* in these private or light verses that
he sometimes, and with increasing frequency as he grew
older, chose the folk form of the ballad stanza or "common
meter" of the hymns and nursery rhymes, and occasionally
even anticipated the dipodic lines that were a common feature of his mature verse—lines that, because they could not
be scanned in terms of the standard feet, fortified the suspicion of his critics that he had no "ear" and so was incapable of writing "correct" verse.[8] The private nature of the

---

blank verse in his senior year at Harvard, when his extracurricular
reading of the pre-Romantics offered him a new model. See, for example, *JMN*, I, p. 261.

In the years between his graduation from college and the achievement of his poetic maturity, Emerson used the form a great deal. Referring to the years 1826-1834, G. W. Allen in *American Prosody*, p.
96, says, "It [that is, blank verse] is used in more poems of his youthful period . . . than any other measure."

For the continuation in this country of the convention of using
neoclassic couplets for public verse until well into the latter half of
the nineteenth century, see Jane Donahue's unpublished doctoral dis-
sertation, " 'Neglected Muse': Neoclassical Forms and Attitudes in
American Poetry from the Connecticut Wits to James Russell Lowell,"
Brown University, 1969.

[8] The dipodic line seems to have been a culturally submerged folk
tradition deriving ultimately from the two-part Anglo-Saxon line
with its two strong stresses before the caesura and at least one of the
two later ones alliterating with the earlier ones, and its irregular number of unstressed syllables. With the substitution of word order for
declension systems that fundamentally altered the language with the
development of Middle English, end rhyme came to take the place of
alliteration, and each half of the long Anglo-Saxon line came to be

verse in his letters seems to have freed him to experiment with forms that appealed to him, perhaps just because they had no "literary" traditions behind them. By the time he was a senior at Harvard, aged seventeen-eighteen and still very far from mature either intellectually or emotionally, Emerson was beginning to attempt verse forms in other conventions than the neoclassic. Blank verse in particular attracted him at this time, though he confined it to his notebooks, still preferring couplets for his public poems. Quite often too by this time he tried his hand at ballad stanzas.

---

considered a separate unit; but the tradition that gave overwhelming importance to stressed syllables (thus making impossible syllable-counting as a method of determining the number and type of feet in a line) and expected very frequent, and stressed, sound-repetitions, continued. Some of the earliest nursery rhymes seem to reflect the buried dipodic tradition. "Old Mother Hubbard," for example, may be written in such a way as to illustrate:

> Old Mother Hubbard
> Went to the cupboard
> To get her poor dog a bone,
> But when she got there
> The cupboard was bare
> And so the poor dog had none.

As arranged above, the first two and the fourth and fifth lines should be read as dipodics rather than as "irregular" examples of either iambic or trochaic dimeter—or any other conventional syllable-counting form.

Most of the books on prosody with which I am familiar do not treat, or even mention, the dipodic rhythm. George R. Stewart, Jr., in *The Technique of English Verse* (New York, Henry Holt, 1930) does treat it, but by trying to fit it into an accentual-syllabic scheme of prosodic analysis, falls into apparent self-contradictions when he finds it characteristic of the simplest folk poetry and yet "the most complicated of all [verse] forms" (p. 83). Henry W. Wells in *New Poets from Old* (New York, Columbia University Press, 1940) surmises its derivation from Anglo-Saxon verse traditions as kept alive in folk memory and finds such later poets as Kipling and Vachel Lindsay using it. The best treatment of dipodics I know of is Lewis Turco's in his *Poetry: An Introduction through Writing* (Reston, Va., Reston Publishing Co., 1973, pp. 127-130, 195-205).

Sometimes his unexpected shifts from the "common meter"
to "long meter" or "short meter," as Watts had distinguished
these variants in his hymnals, suggest that the hymns the
Emerson children had been required to memorize and recite at home were a more direct inspiration than the folk
ballads he was only now becoming acquainted with. The
influence of the hymn forms on Emerson's mature poetry
has been too little recognized. It would require little if any
exaggeration to say that nothing that Emerson learned in
childhood was ever forgotten—just radically reinterpreted.
The following stanza from what is probably his earliest
extant poem, a hymn entitled "The Sabbath" that may have
been written when he was nine, has more of the ring of his
most characteristic mature poetry than the smoothest
pentameter couplets of his youth ever do—

> Remember your Redeemer's love,
> And meditate on things above,
> Forsake while you are here below,
> The path that leads to realms of woe.

Less regular four-stress couplets than these would be the
verse form he most commonly chose in his maturity. The
form combines the prosody of "long meter" hymns with the
couplet rhyming preferred by the neoclassic masters and
his school teachers and college tutors. Some forty years earlier Blake had turned to Watts and the folk ballads as an
escape from reigning neoclassic conventions, though Emerson at the time had no way of knowing that there was a
precedent for what he was doing. He was repeating the
Romantic experience on his own, independently and with
much fumbling.

In all ways, including finding his own voice as a poet, Emerson's maturity came unusually late. Nothing that I have said
so far is meant to suggest that the large body of verse he
wrote between the ages of ten and eighteen marks him as

a precocious genius among poets. Verse-writing was encouraged in school and at home, for one thing, and for another, much of Emerson's earliest verse is plainly crude, while even the best of it seems just what it is, the work of a clever boy. Its chief interest today lies in the demonstration it affords that he was perfectly capable of writing "correctly" and "smoothly" when he was writing imitatively. Such distinction was sufficient to provide a realistic basis for his ambition to become a poet, however he might earn his living.

What I have distinguished as the "serious" or "public" verse is generally too imitative and immature to be worth reading today, except as we may find it mildly interesting to watch the poet who would later write "Merlin" doing finger exercises in technique. One of the verse entries in his college theme notebook for 1819-1821 is a fair illustration. The technical handling of the pentameter couplets is perfectly competent in its derivative way, and the lines have a certain fluency, but there is nothing in either their manner or their matter to suggest that they were written by the Emerson we know.

> Oh there are times when the celestial muse
> Will bless the dull with inspiration's dews,—
> Will bid the clowns gross sluggish soul expand
> And catch one rapturous glimpse of Fairy Land
> 'Tis when descending fancy, from the bowers
> Of blest Elysium seeks this world of ours
> In wayward freak the glittering goddess flies
> To make some haunt an earthly paradise
> With all her various train in trackless flight
> She comes at merry morn or deep midnight.

A few lines from two earlier "public" poems on which Emerson seems to have worked hard to satisfy adult expectations of the time will suffice to exhibit the technical expertness and conventional ideas of his most serious boyhood verse. "Lines on Washington . . ." dates from 1814, when he was eleven years old, and "Poetical Essay" from

1815. The first opens with the following two couplets and continues predictably:

> In former years when Britain rul'd these States
> And like a tyrant doom'd our hapless fates
> The God of Israel heard our groans and cries
> And bade to life A WASHINGTON arise.

"Poetical Essay" achieves a somewhat more faithful imitation of the Popean high neoclassic style with its capitalized abstractions and its concluding antithetically balanced line, though it mostly ignores the convention of the medial caesura:

> When dread Ambition first her flag unfurl'd
> And taught her sons to subjugate the world,
> A god decreed in mercy to mankind,
> O thought most worthy of the mighty mind!
> That Independence should descend to Earth,
> Goddess divine! of high immortal birth;
> With laurel crown'd, in majesty array'd,
> From Ida's top descends the heavenly maid;
> Where'eer Ambition spread her influence round,
> Where'eer her sons the brazen trumpet sound,
> There Independence rais'd her silver star,
> And led to Peace through Battle, Blood, and War.

These and a great many similar verses demonstrate, it seems to me, in addition to an acquaintance with the conventions being followed, a high level of verbal ability for a boy so young and a sensitive ear for the rhythms of the prosodic form. The form, considered simply as a given set of conventions, is well, but not slavishly, handled. The "inspiration" of course is entirely *ab extra*, to paraphrase Emerson's later praise of the teachings of Jesus because they came, he said, *ab intra*. Considering the poet's age when he wrote them, we can agree, I should think, that they at least show promise of literary achievement to come.

When he was not imitating Pope, Emerson sometimes, just before and after his graduation from college, imitated the Graveyard School, particularly Gray himself. The blank verse of the following lines—somewhat suggestive of Bryant's in "Thanatopsis," but less distinguished I should say—shows him adopting a post-Popean form, but the ideas might have come from any one, or several, of dozens of sources. "The Grave" dates from the year after his graduation from college, but it does not differ noticeably from much of the verse he had been writing a year or two earlier:

> Can thy gates shut, Oh City of the Dead!
> And cease to add the eternal increment
> Which crowds thy caverns from the worlds of life?
> God spreads beneath us the enveloping gulf
> And feeds its fill and gnashing gluttony
> With our poor shrinking tenements of clay.
> Who hath gone down inquisitive to see
> Thy ribbed vaults, thy drear magnificence
> The thrones of Death and Darkness, or to make
> Acquaintance with thy countless colonies
> Heirs to thy strength, dark subjects of thy sway?
> Ask not, frail man, it boots thee not to know,
> Myriads have sought, thyself shall speedily seek
> In thy own turn the abysses of the pit
> Whose silent horror tempts thee to be bold.

Not content with apostrophizing the grave, he wrote a poem "To Melancholy"—and thought well enough of it to revise and improve it later. Sometimes he versified the history he was reading, sometimes he tried on medieval ascetic ideas in blank verse. Ideas and verse forms alike reflected almost immediately whatever he was reading at the time that excited him, which more often than not proved to be reading done in time stolen from his prescribed studies.

The verse he wrote in his letters seems to me, as I have said, more interesting on the whole than the verse he must have taken more seriously and certainly worked harder on. On the lowest level of interest we have the remarkably facile versifying of his 1814 verse letter to Sarah Alden

Bradford, written at age eleven, which concludes, after describing what he had seen during a visit to a museum,

> Here stopping though much more I might relate
> I leave these lines in their unfinish'd state
> Though few they are and many faults you see
> Pardon them all and quickly write to me.

More interesting because the cleverness is more complicated is an 1816 letter to Edward that parodies the substance of Gray's "Elegy" in the verse form of Pope, then,
with a hasty transition ("But oh Urania at thy shrine I bow /
And ask thy pardon for digression now!") becomes a parody
of Ossian.

The parodies and nonsense verse of the letters to Edward
and William are full of humor, high spirits, and frequently
successful wit, exhibiting a side of Emerson's nature that
finds rarer and much more subtle expression in the mature
poetry, discernible in tone only, or in the intellectual play-
fulness inherent in paradoxy. An 1817 letter to Edward, for
example, strikes me as continuously interesting in the delicate and shifting balance it maintains between the serious
and the playful as it dilates on the subjects of Hope and
Despair. Its opening lines prepare us for nonsense:

> Dear Ned, I promis'd some time since, you know,
> That my next letter should all news forego,
> And wholly fill'd by 'sentiment' and taste
> On common stuff should, no black fluid, waste:
> Then why should not Apollo fill the sheet
> And I repair to his Castalian seat?
> Yes, I'm resolved, in measur'd verse to write—
> But stop—the subject?—any thing that's right.

But if Waldo (as he was by this time signing his letters, having dropped "Ralph") thought he was writing conventional
nonsense in the following lines, we, reading them, may be
moved to wonder whether we have a right to take them as
foreshadowing the mature writer who would give affirma-

tive endings to such "dark" essays as "Experience," "Montaigne, or the Skeptic," and "Fate":

Yes, Edward, we shall find as on we go,
In life's all-varying scenes of Joy, and woe,
That when the clouds of Sorrow and Distress
The thickest join in Life's dull wilderness,
Then Hope is strongest. . . .

But it is not only in the letters that we find light verse full of verve and imaginative high jinks. In the Notebooks too the verses presumably meant only for Emerson's own eyes are often much like those he wrote to his brothers. He imitates a medieval ballad, writes a poem entitled "Something Silly," or makes verse notes for a comic class poem in Hudibrastics, doubtless to be enjoyed by the Pythologian Club. He writes comic stanzas in bouncy tetrameters, a drinking song—again, apparently, for the enjoyment of his fellow Pythologians—urging, appropriately enough in view of its intended use,

Drink brothers drink the wine flows fast
The tutors are near and the daylight's past.

He writes a pure nonsense song and tries his hand at an anagram. Clearly, he is amusing himself and at the same time testing his power to handle a variety of forms.

Emerson's poetic apprenticeship lasted almost a quarter of a century, from age nine or ten until he was approaching his middle thirties. Not only the school and college verses but most of those he wrote in the first several years after graduation seem the work of a writer who has not yet found his own identity. But reading them should correct some common notions about how Emerson became a poet and why he wrote the way he did in his maturity.

Though graduation from college brought no sudden maturity to his verse, still it is possible to detect a slight change

occurring in the verse Emerson now confined mostly to his
Notebooks. More frequently in the 1820's the verses seem
to have been written solely to please himself rather than
one of his mentors or both himself and one of his brothers.
Now he felt freer to write as he wished, experimenting
more boldly with new verse forms recently encountered in
his reading and trying on the new ideas that, no thanks to
Harvard's curriculum, were coming to him. With a sure
sense of what was beginning to happen to his horizons and
to his sense of his own unexplored potentials, he started a
new set of Notebooks entitled collectively "Wide World."
In 1822 in "Wide World 6" he wrote down some lines that
suggest the kind of "wideness" his imaginative world was
beginning to have. Both in verse form and in their imagery
the lines may well be the earliest clear foreshadowing of the
best and most characteristic poetry of Emerson's maturity:

> There the Northern light reposes
>   With ruddy flames in circles bright
> Like a wreath of ruby roses
>   On the dusky brow of night.

But though these lines might well have been written in
the 1830's or even later, their maturity suggests the transitional character of the verse Emerson wrote in the 1820's
rather than any abrupt leap beyond boyhood versifying.
The neoclassic forms which up to now had been his chief
resource continued to predominate for a while yet, but attempts at other forms increased in frequency. The influence
of the British pre-Romantics and Wordsworth becomes
more apparent not only in the blank verse and stanzaic
forms he now frequently substitutes for end-stopped couplets but in the appearance of new ideas and attitudes. In his
senior year he had copied passages from Wordsworth into
his notebooks but not until a year or so later would he write
any verse of his own that suggested Wordsworth's, and
even then, in "Good-bye," the influence of the pre-Romantics is still very apparent. In these years he tried his hand
at modified Spenserian stanzas, worked sporadically at a

Gothic tale in prose, a genre for which, all too clearly, he had no talent at all, and versified his reading in Scott. He imitated the Graveyard School in poems entitled "The Grave" and "To Melancholy," and even, with apparently no suspicion that his was not a dramatic imagination, tried writing dramatic blank verse all too clearly modeled on Shakespeare's. (If the result was not noticeably Shakespearean in effect, at least it showed he could versify as smoothly in blank verse as he had proved he could in couplets: "Here build a temple of eternal fame" cannot be faulted on prosodic grounds.) But the experiments of the period just before and just after graduation did not prevent him from falling back on the form that had served him so well for so long to compose a twenty-four line poem on the theme expressed in one of its pentameter couplets:

> We look for days of joy and groves of peace
> Where all the turmoils of ambition cease.

The "ambition" that had played so prominent a role among his motives for versifying did not suddenly desert him. He still wanted to distinguish himself in some way and still thought of poetry as the chief possibility, more attractive to him now, he thought, than its early rival, oratory. The new element in his situation in the years just after graduation was the sense of freedom to explore both the world and his own resources, to establish his own identity in a world that began to seem much wider and more unknown than he had realized. If he were going to write to please himself, he would have to find out first who he was, what he believed, what his tastes were. It is not surprising that in these years he often explored blind alleys and tried on attitudes and ideas that strike us as thoroughly "unEmersonian." During the earliest years of the twenties he sometimes wrote verse that, as in these lines from the long poem "Arthur's Dream" on which he worked intermittently, sound a bit like early Tennyson:

> Who are they that in blood red robes
> Like giants cross the dusky plain?

Trying his hand at another "poetic" form, the Gothic prose tale already mentioned, he suggests Poe, though Poe would have been unlikely to break into verses written in long and common meter in the middle of his tale, as Emerson did in his "Magician Story." (When the youthful Emerson sounds most like Poe, he always sounds like very bad Poe.) Incidents from "Arthur's Dream" and "Magician Story" were apparently reused in an abortive attempt to combine Gothic melodrama and ballad forms in "King Richard's Death: A Ballad." "The Maniac's Verse," written in the winter after his graduation and technically mature as verse, again shows him trying on a Gothic mask for fit, though only a few months earlier he had fallen back on the tried and trusted pentameter couplet for the first version of his "Valedictory Poem." By 1821-1822 the gap between the verse Emerson intended for public occasions and his private experiments in his Notebooks was wider than ever. Really finding himself as a poet would require the reduction of that gap. By the end of the decade, he had made considerable progress in that direction, though not until he had reached his middle thirties would he really accomplish it.

Something of the distance and general direction of the poetic journey Emerson travelled in the decade after graduation is suggested by the contrast between some lines from what can only be called a "conventional romantic lyric" he wrote probably in 1822 and some others he wrote in 1827. The "un-Emersonian" quality of the 1822 lines is transparent:

> I spread my gorgeous sail
> Upon a starless sea
> And o'er the deep with a chilly gale
> My painted bark sailed fast & free.

In the unpolished blank verse of the 1827 fragment we find Emerson saying something he really meant—or was beginning to discover he meant—and foreshadowing, however faintly, some of the central ideas in both his own later "Mer-

lin" and Thoreau's "Inspiration," though the voice we hear
stating the ideas sounds more like that of "Thanatopsis"
than like the voice of Emerson's maturity:

> When thy soul
> Is filled with a just image fear not thou
> Lest halting rhymes or unharmonious verse
> Cripple the fair Conception Leave the heart
> Alone to find its language. In all tongues
> It hath a sovereign instinct that doth teach
> An eloquence which rules can never give.
> In the high hour when Destiny ordains
> That thou bear testimony to its dooms
> That hour a guiding spirit shall impart
> The fervid utterance art could never find
> Wait then, stern friend, wait in majestic peace.

Perhaps four lines he apparently wrote on December 21
of 1827 and left unfinished suggest even better the road
Emerson as poet was travelling in these years. The lines in
question follow immediately after three stanzas of nature
description written in fairly regular tetrameters, though in
the last line of the third stanza he shifts to pentameter
("And poised his broad wings on the morning air"):

> And I am here
> On the green earth contemplating the moon
> Much marvelling what may betide tomorrow
> I love my life

Granted that the lines are rough, hardly more than notes
for what might become a poem, still the voice we hear in
them is Emerson's own voice. Abandoning what he must
have felt as the effort to express his new perceptions and
feelings in regular meters, he now ignores conventional
prosody altogether to bring to true expression his sense of
wonder, mystery, and possibility. Only the moon seems bor-
rowed from poetic convention. There is a sense in which
these unstructured lines give fuller expression to Emerson's
developing poetic sensibility than do those of "Good-bye,"
which he had written half a dozen years before, starting off

with a Wordsworthian thought but developing it in language that owes more to Wordsworth's predecessors than to Wordsworth until the last line, when we hear what sounds like Emerson's own voice:

GOOD-BYE, proud world! I'm going home:
Thou art not my friend, and I'm not thine.
Long through thy weary crowds I roam;
A river-ark on the ocean brine,
Long I've been tossed like the driven foam;
But now, proud world! I'm going home.

Good-bye to Flattery's fawning face;
To Grandeur with his wise grimace;
To upstart Wealth's averted eye;
To supple Office, low and high;
To crowded halls, to court and street;
To frozen hearts and hasting feet;
To those who go, and those who come;
Good-bye, proud world! I'm going home.

I am going to my hearth-stone,
Bosomed in yon green hills alone,—
A secret nook in a pleasant land,
Whose groves the frolic fairies planned;
Where arches green the livelong day,
Echo the blackbird's roundelay,
And vulgar feet have never trod
A spot that is sacred to thought and God.

O, when I am safe in my sylvan home,
I tread on the pride of Greece and Rome;
And when I am stretched beneath the pines,
Where the evening star so holy shines,
I laugh at the lore and the pride of man,
At the sophist schools and the learned clan;
For what are they all, in their high conceit,
When man in the bush with God may meet?[9]

It was no doubt the conventionally acceptable quality of "Good-Bye" that made it the earliest of his "juvenilities" he chose to send out for publication. But that its acceptability

[9] *Poems*, pp. 3-4.

was achieved in part at least by a betrayal of his own feelings seems to be implied by the way he apologized for it to
the editor to whom he sent it: The lines, he said, "have a
slight misanthropy, a shade deeper than belongs to me.
. . ."[10] But just as uncharacteristic of his maturity as their
"misanthropy" is the tendency they betray to think in
abstractions.

As Emerson was beginning to think his own thoughts and
feel his own feelings, so he was beginning to wait upon
what he called, in lines written in 1824, "an unlaurelled
muse." Neither the decision to do something different from
what he had learned to do very competently in school and
college nor the resultant change in the kind of verse he normally wrote was, as I have said, sudden and sure; slow,
hesitant, vacillating rather. The decision and the change
cannot be dated in any one year. Even in college he had
once chafed at the "prison" of rhyme (probably having
couplets in mind), and when in 1824 he announced his preference for "an unlaurelled muse" he still used the pentameter couplets that had served him so well so long for
purely derivative verse.

> Safe in their ancient crannies dark & deep
> Let kings & conquerors saints & soldiers sleep.
> Late in the world too late perchance for fame
> Just late enough to reap abundant blame
> I choose a novel theme, a bold abuse
> Of critic charters, an unlaurelled muse.
>
> Old mouldy men & books & names & lands
> Disgust my reason & defile my hands
> I had as lief respect an ancient shoe
> As love Old things for age, & hate the new.
> I spurn the Past, my mind disdains its nod
> Nor kneels in homage to so mean a god.

We may assume, I think, that it was habit and not thoughtful choice that made Emerson announce his preference for
an unlaurelled muse in the verse form that in his time and

10 *Ibid.*, p. 403.

place, and in his own mind, was more thoroughly be-
laurelled than any other.

Nevertheless, if his poetic growth to maturity strikes us
as unusually slow and uncertain in direction, the signs that
it was occurring are clear enough in the notebook verse of
the later 1820's. One such sign is what may appear to be
simply "carelessness" but should rather, I think, be interpreted as evidence of an increasing desire for freedom from
the restraints of what he was beginning to think of as arbitrary conventions: shifting verse forms in the middle of
poems, for example, from pentameter to tetrameter or vice
versa, occurs ever more frequently as the decade goes on.
(Now and then, throwing aside all restraints, he wrote what
he once called "prose run mad," but more frequently he
permitted himself only these *little* liberties.) More significant is the increasing frequency with which he turned to a
rough tetrameter in which the achievement of regular
prosody or rhyme no longer seems to be the controlling mo-
tive. The following unrhymed tetrameter lines written late
in 1824 lamenting his lack of poetic power will illustrate:

> My pulse is slow my blood is cold
> My stammering tongue is rudely tuned.

Two bits of verse on facing pages of the *JMN* for late
1827 give a clearer indication of the direction Emerson's
muse would take in a few more years. The tetrameter lines
on the "blackbird" (redwing?) are awkward and halting, to
be sure, but certainly there is more imaginative life and a
more personal voice in them than there is in the smoothly
conventional sonnet, "Written in Sickness," he wrote just a
few days later. A part of the celebration of the blackbird's
song goes like this:

> There tilting & shaking down the dew
> Sang his good song the merry blackbird
> Quoth he, I hope you like music young man—
> For I'm determined to be heard.

And straightway as he sang, the sound
Woke every bird in the silent woods
On a thousand sprays, above around
They poured their notes to the sylvan gods.

The lines needed more work, of course, but in the concreteness of their imagery and in the prosodic shift of the third
line we have suggestions of Emerson's best mature style.

Two poems to Ellen that Emerson included in *Poems*
(1847), "To Ellen at the South" and "To Ellen," both written
in 1829, may serve as a convenient indicator of the degree
of poetic "self-reliance" and maturity Emerson had arrived
at by the end of the twenties. Neither poem, clearly, is one
of his best. Both are conventionally structured in general,
both contain a rather large amount of conventional poetic
diction, and both might conceivably have been written by
some other poet of the time. Yet both poems strike me as
attractive and readable minor love lyrics and each of them,
especially "To Ellen at the South," contains several outstanding lines and images that have the Emersonian ring to
them. "To Ellen at the South" also suggests the mature
Emerson in its prosodic irregularity: it begins with dipodic
lines, then shifts in the third stanza to what would be describable as Common Meter were it not for the additional
rhyme, then moves back and forth erratically between
dipodics, Short Meter, and Long Meter:

> The green grass is bowing,
>   The morning wind is in it;
> 'T is a tune worth thy knowing,
>   Though it change every minute.
>
> 'T is a tune of the Spring;
>   Every year plays it over
> To the robin on the wing,
>   And to the pausing lover.
>
> O'er ten thousand, thousand acres,
>   Goes light the nimble zephyr;
> The Flowers—tiny sect of Shakers—
>   Worship him ever.

Hark to the winning sound!
   They summon thee, dearest, —
Saying, 'We have dressed for thee the ground,
   Nor yet thou appearest.

'O hasten;' 't is our time,
   Ere yet the red Summer
Scorch our delicate prime,
   Loved of bee, — the tawny hummer.

'O pride of thy race!
   Sad, in sooth, it were to ours,
If our brief tribe miss thy face
   We poor New England flowers.

'Fairest, choose the fairest members
   Of our lithe society;
June's glories and September's
   Show our love and piety.

'Thou shalt command us all, —
   April's cowslip, summer's clover,
To the gentian in the fall
   Blue-eyed pet of blue-eyed lover.

'O come, then, quickly come!
   We are budding, we are blowing;
And the wind that we perfume
   Sings a tune that's worth the knowing.'[11]

That "tiny sect of Shakers" is both "good Emerson" and good proto-Dickinson.

"To Ellen" is prosodically much more regular and its diction more generalized. Its "Past" and "Hope," "Mirth" and "Flattery," and "Love" and "Reason" seem a carry-over from Emerson's apprenticeship in neoclassic and pre-Romantic forms. Its sturdy tetrameter lines though still manage to give the impression of marching along with the years and the thought as if no poetic convention were controlling them:

[11] *Ibid.*, pp. 93-94.

And Ellen, when the graybeard years
    Have brought us to life's evening hour,
And all the crowded Past appears
    A tiny scene of sun and shower,

Then, if I read the page aright
    Where Hope, the soothsayer, reads our lot,
Thyself shalt own the page was bright,
    Well that we loved, woe had we not.

When Mirth is dumb and Flattery's fled,
    And mute thy music's dearest tone,
When all but Love itself is dead
    And all but deathless Reason gone.[12]

If neither of these poems, which, except for "Good-bye,"
I take to be the most sustained and best of all the poetic efforts we have glanced at so far in surveying Emerson's ap-
prentice verse, is comparable to his best poems of a half a
dozen years later, it may be not so much that they are
"early" as that the theme of romantic love—however dearly
he loved Ellen—did not then and never would stir Emerson's imaginative powers in the way meditating on "the conduct of life" or on the relation of the "each" to the "All" did.
To be deeply moved, his imagination required that there
be a moral or a metaphysical dimension somewhere in the
subject. It is no accident that it is in "Each and All" and
"The Problem," both published in 1839, that we first hear
the characteristic voice of Emerson's best mature writing
coming through in clear and strong accents.

It was of course not simply poetic maturity but intellectual
and (I suspect) psychic maturity too that came to Emerson
only in his and the century's third decade. Now out of the
ministry, in which he had increasingly felt himself something of a misfit, he was in effect a lay preacher with the
lecture platform for his pulpit and Lyceum audiences for

[12] *Ibid.*, pp. 94-95.

his congregation, and he could devote himself wholeheartedly to self-discovery and self-definition. He entered his most creative period in the middle thirties with a much keener sense than ever before of what he wanted to do and what he didn't, and what he could do and what he couldn't. Not surprisingly, his new certainty about who and what he was and what his work would be coincided chronologically with the achievement of his own poetic voice. Hereafter there would be no more attempts at witty neoclassic couplets, at Poe-esque Gothic tales in prose or verse, at pretty romantic lyrics.

The verse of the early thirties is still as clearly "transitional" in character as I have called the verse of the twenties. "A Letter," which dates from 1831 but reminds us of the verse epistles Emerson had begun to write more than twenty years earlier, will illustrate. Except for the short second and thirteenth lines, its blank verse is quite regular and fluent, there is a minimal use of the inversions of word order that would become a marked feature of the later verse, and the lines do not so much announce, as Saadi or Merlin might, as expound and explain. Yet the poem strikes me as distinctly better (though Emerson chose not to publish it) than "Good-bye," which expresses a similar theme. The voice in it is only intermittently his own, to be sure, but there is more concreteness in the imagery, more of a sense of place, more daring use of the "non-poetic," as in the line that breaks the meter to name the counties and in that most unpoetic of images, the thermometer:

> Dear brother, would you know the life,
> Please God, that I would lead?
> On the first wheels that quit this weary town
> Over yon western bridges I would ride
> And with a cheerful benison forsake
> Each street and spire and roof, incontinent.
> Then would I seek where God might guide my steps,
> Deep in a woodland tract, a sunny farm,
> Amid the mountain counties, Hants, Franklin, Berks,

Where down the rock ravine a river roars,
Even from a brook, and where old woods
Not tamed and cleared cumber the ground
With their centennial wrecks.
Find me a slope where I can feel the sun
And mark the rising of the early stars.
There will I bring my books, — my household gods,
The reliquaries of my dead saint, and dwell
In the sweet odor of her memory.
Then in the uncouth solitude unlock
My stock of art, plant dials in the grass,
Hang in the air a bright thermometer
And aim a telescope at the inviolate sun.[13]

The man whose ideal self-image called upon him to be a "voyager of light and noon" is beginning to discover himself in these lines, but he is not yet quite his own man as a poet. What should a poet do aside from going apart to seek God by looking at the stars and studying the source of light with the best instruments of modern knowledge?

It is possible to trace in the quotations and ideas Emerson put into his Notebooks the gradual evolution of his mature idea of the true poet's role. As early as 1826 or 1827 he had copied into one of his "Blotting Books" a sentence from the *Satyricon* of Petronius Arbiter: "Precipitandus est liber spiritus," which may be translated "the free spirit must plunge headlong."[14] Plunging headlong, poetically—which would require self-trust and a certain disregard both of conventions and of the possible consequences of ignoring them—had certainly not been characteristic of the bulk of Emerson's verse up to this time. Again in 1827 in the same "Blotting Book" he put down a thought of his own that would lead him ultimately to try to achieve in his verse and to recommend in his lectures and essays an "innocent eye," a fresh way of seeing: "If men had never been children I fear there would be no such thing as poetry."[15] Finally, an entry that the editors of *JMN* can date only as having been

13 *Ibid.*, pp. 391-392. 14 *JMN*, VI, p. 60. 15 *Ibid.*, p. 69.

made sometime between 1824 and 1836, but that strikes me
as having the ring of the thirties more than of the twenties,
will serve to suggest another idea about poetry that was to
have lasting consequences for the later verse: "The poem
is made up of lines each of which filled the sky of the poet
in its turn. So that mere synthesis produces a work quite
super human."[16] (Of course, what Emerson here belittles as
"mere synthesis" would often prove quite beyond his
powers.)

To the extent to which Emerson's mature verse is unmis-
takably his own, impossible to think of as having been written by the more successful and representative poets of the
day—by Tennyson in England, for example, or by Longfellow in the United States—insofar as it eludes or violates
the norms of Romantic, Victorian, and "Modernist" poetry
alike, Emerson's verse illustrates his willingness to "plunge,"
to write out of his own ideas of what poetry should be.[17]
Most of his best and most typical verse after the middle
thirties would either assume and imply, or else develop as
a theme, the necessity of cultivating the childlike eye that
sees all things newly and so with wonder. And it would remain true of the bulk of his verse—with the notable exception of course of his very best poems, as I shall try to show
—that separate lines or couplets would be more memorable
than the shape, the design, of whole poems, as his detractors have so often charged and his admirers usually ad-

[16] *Ibid.*, p. 225.

[17] Carl F. Strauch, who has studied Emerson's poetry longer and
more carefully than anyone else, has traced the origins of Emerson's
mature ideas of what poetry should be and do in his important article "The Mind's Voice . . ." cited previously. He finds behind Emerson's mature ideal and best practice Sampson Reed, the Swedenborgian
("correspondences"), Coleridge (the Bardic ideal), Anglo-Saxon (runic verse), Wordsworth (the truncated blank verse line), and Milton
(the catalogue line in blank verse), as well as neo-Platonism and other
influences that affected his thought and style. Writing from a somewhat different point of view and out of different resources from my
own, Strauch arrives at generally similar conclusions. His article
seems to me so nearly definitive that whenever I am aware of differing
with it I shall note the fact and give my reasons.

mitted—a trait not very surprising in the work of a poet who thought of verse as fashioned from lines each of which was the product of a distinct intuition or epiphany. A great many of those who care for Emerson's verse at all can recite "In vain produced, all rays return; / Evil will bless, and ice will burn," but how many can recall clearly the design and argument of "Uriel" as a whole? Yet "Uriel" surely is one of his best poems.

Not all of Emerson's mature verse, of course, has the stylistic characteristics of "Uriel," "Brahma," or "The Sphinx." His occasional poems and hymns—"Boston," for example, or "The Concord Hymn" and "The Boston Hymn"—had a different purpose and were written in a different mode. Furthermore, as has been so often, and rightly, said, Emerson's mature poetic theory was always both more consistent and more radical than his practice. Nevertheless, many of the characteristic formal features of his mature verse are implicit in the notebook jottings I have quoted. His characteristic tetrameter couplets or stanzas, with their frequent and emphatic rhymes, are functional in verse conceived as a collection (ideally, a "synthesis") of discrete intuitions. Although it has always seemed to many of its readers to be deficient in dignity, musical potential, and flow, the rhymed tetrameter line, in either couplet or quatrain form, has advantages for a poet whose overriding purpose is to render flashes of insight memorable. Again, the unusual frequency with which Emerson used folk verse forms, particularly in the poems he left unfinished and so did not publish during his lifetime, may remind us of the connection he saw between children and poetry. For the traditional forms of nursery rhymes, singing games, ballads, and hymns were meant for and appreciated by actual children or "child-like" adults—earlier, supposedly less "sophisticated" adults, in the case of the ballads, or "simple, uncritical" believers, in the case of the hymns.[18] Even the way Emerson treated the

[18] Strauch's failure to consider the folk forms as an influence on Emerson's mature style seems to me an oversight. The passage Strauch cites from Coleridge's Preface to "Christabel," explaining that

conventions of the established forms, whether folk or literary, his cavalier disregard for consistency in metrical patterns, and his imperfect or even missing rhymes, may be
seen as appropriate enough to a poetic ideal that sets the
highest value on recklessness, the child's perception, and
intuition.

In the final years of the thirties Emerson was beginning
to work out the ideas of the poet's nature and role and, less
clearly, of his method and manner, that would find expression in the essay "The Poet" several years later. His conceptions of the poet's proper method and manner, however un-
developed they were and, in large part, would remain, were
clear enough in their general drift so far as they went. The
poet should utilize the natural and inherent symbolism of
language itself to go beyond the communicative possibilities of ordinary language, attempting to arouse in the reader an intuition similar to his own of the spiritual realities
and laws hidden from custom-blinded eyes within and behind the flux of actual forms. And he should do this by let-
ting nature speak through him, using him as a conduit or
spokesman. When poems were written this way, the "argument" or intent of a poem would create its own form. The
form of the ideal poem would be organic, growing as a
plant does by laws within itself that make it itself and not
something else.

---

the meter is not "irregular" but founded on a "new principle" in
which only accents, not syllables, are counted may well have influenced Emerson, and certainly shows Coleridge rediscovering the folk
tradition before Emerson did, but Emerson, as I see it, did not need
Coleridge at this point, as he did for more philosophic matters. His
childhood had thoroughly steeped him in folk traditions in versifying,
and his developing ideas would have made it natural for him to value
folk forms even if Coleridge had never explained the prosody of
"Christabel" as he did or if Emerson had never read the explanation.
I might add that it seems to me that Emerson made a much more
creative, frequent, and, at his best, successful use of folk forms than
Coleridge did, "The Rime of the Ancient Mariner" excepted.

The conception of "organic form," not only as Emerson expressed it but in the expression of later exponents, strikes me as more a suggestive metaphor than a precise definition—and a metaphor of which Emerson himself was sometimes a victim, as Whitman would be later—but despite its vagueness it surely seems to point toward "free verse" as the ideal. It would be left to Whitman to see and practice this implication of organic theory, but sometimes in the privacy of the notebooks in the late years of the decade Emerson seemed to be approaching it. Perhaps instead of concluding that the notebook drafts of poems are as a rule simply "bad" verse, though often of course they are just that, we might think of them as more "self-reliant" and uncompromising verse than that which Emerson chose to put before the public. The opening lines of "O darling spring" (1838), for instance, seem to me to suggest Whitman's later practice both in matter and in manner:

> O darling spring languishing
> Makes all things softly smile
> Makes pictures of all
> Justifying the young man in leaving his affairs
> Making all drunk with a draught of lilies
> Making the young girls sweeter
> & making the youths almost women.

On the other hand, some of the notebook drafts of poems in these years seem less like experiments in free verse than like symptoms of Emerson's tendency to weaken the conventional boundaries between prose and verse. This is the way the first draft of "The Snow-Storm" appears in an 1834 notebook. The images are here, the guiding idea, and even whole lines just as they would be used in the poem, but the passage as a whole seems to exist somewhere in a no man's land between poetic prose and blank verse.

> Announced by all the trumpets of the winds Arrived
> the snow & driving o'er the field, seems nowhere to alight.

The whited air hides hills & woods, the river & the heaven
& veils the farmhouse at the garden's end. The traveller
stopped & sled the courier's feet delayed all friends shut
out the housemates sit Around the radiant fireplace en-
closed in a tumultuous privacy of storm. Come see the
Northwind's masonry out of an unseen quarry evermore fur-
nished with tile the fierce artificer carves a white bastion
with projected roof round every windward stake & tree &
door speeding the myriad-handed his wild work so fanciful
so savage nought cares he for number or proportion mock-
ingly on coop & kennel he hangs Parian wreaths A swan-
like form invests the hidden thorn Fills up the farmer's
lane from wall to wall maugre the farmer's sighs & at the
gates a tapering turret overtops the work

Then when his hours are numbered & the world is all his
own Retiring as he were not Leaves when the sun appears
astonished art to ape in his slow structures stone by stone
Built in an age the mad wind's night work The frolic archi-
tecture of the snow.[19]

In his printed verse, as in his life generally, Emerson
compromised—or, to use a less derogatory word, found a
middle ground—between his radical ideas and his natural
prudence. Refusing, characteristically, to be tightly bound
by recognized conventions in poetry, he stopped short of
renouncing them entirely. Doing so while continuing to
write verse would have required that he create a radically
new form or forms to replace the discarded old ones—if,
as I assume, poetry is never properly to be described as
"formless." But for this, as things turned out for him, he
generally found himself lacking the time or the energy, or
both. Only in his best poems did he break sufficiently free
from the rationalistic forms he had mastered in the years
of his apprenticeship to forge a personal style wholly adequate to the expression of his vision.[20] By the time his first

19 *JMN*, VI, p. 246.
20 Rejecting the idea of Stephen Whicher and others that Emerson
remained bound throughout his poetic career by the inappropriate
eighteenth-century verse forms learned in his youth, Strauch argues

volume of verse was published late in 1846, his early ambition of achieving fame as a poet (in the sense at least of one
who makes verses) had been much weakened by a growing
recognition that it was his destiny to be most often, and perhaps most effectively, a poet when he spoke from the platform or through his essays, in sibylline and metaphoric
prose.

---

that the forms of Emerson's poems are, instead, "Romantic, Old
English, Bardic, . . . Neo-Platonic." Each of these two views, Whicher's
and Strauch's, seems to me to need qualification, Whicher's seeming
better to account for much of the least successful verse, Strauch's for
the triumphs. See "The Mind's Voice . . . ," pp. 52-53.

CHAPTER III

The Achievement of the Poems:
"Artful Thunder"

By the early 1830's, then, when he himself was about thirty, Emerson had proved that he could make prosodically "smooth" and "correct" verses in several traditional forms of "measured language," but he had not yet written any whole poems that would make him seem worth remembering today as anything more than one of the minor versifiers of the period. A decade earlier in "Good-bye" he had achieved a sufficiently craftsmanlike blending of Wordsworthian sentiments and language with echoes of Wordsworth's predecessors to cast doubt on the seldom-questioned judgment of his nineteenth-century critics that though he had the "soul" of a poet he lacked technical competence and a poetic "ear"; but the poem considered as a poem rather than as an exercise in versifying strikes me as adding nothing to Gray and subtracting something from Wordsworth. Even "A Letter," written in 1831, strongly suggests the major poems to come only in its last few lines. Emerson arrived at intellectual and poetic maturity at the same time, in the middle and later thirties, when the ideas he had long been gathering from such diverse sources as Plato and George Fox, the Cambridge Platonists and Coleridge, his seventeenth-century favorites and Swedenborg, finally sank in and began to coalesce. If he has any claim today to be considered among the greater American poets, as I think he has, that claim must rest primarily on the dozen or more strongest poems he wrote chiefly in the decade between 1836 and 1846.

Several of his finest poems, including "Each and All" and "The Problem," appear to date from the late thirties, but the three greatest, as I read the verse, "Merlin," "Bacchus," and

"Hamatreya," all seem to have been written in 1845-1846, when the approaching publication of his first volume of poems prompted a brief but intense period of renewed concentration on the form of writing in which he had first hoped to gain fame. All three poems are prosodically and otherwise unconventional by the standards of their time. The best poems written later than this, including "Days," "The Titmouse," and "Terminus," tend to take fewer liberties with the "rules" of mid-nineteenth-century versification. "Brahma," 1857, is a very traditional poem formally, while the next year's "The Adirondacs" is written in the perfectly conventional blank verse Emerson had long before shown himself capable of producing. Despite the fine new poems Emerson's second collection contained, Browning's judgment of *May-Day and Other Pieces*, that the new book added nothing really new to what Emerson had to contribute as a poet, seems to me essentially sound.[1] Emerson's most creative period came late and lasted only a dozen years or so.

How significant then is Emerson's achievement in his best poems? What shall we think about the quality of the bulk of his verse? Why are his weaker poems weak, if they are weak? How many of his widely agreed-upon "faults" as a poet are really faults? Only "judicial criticism," presumably, can attempt to answer such questions, but the recent experience of reading straight through more than a century of accumulated critical judgments of Emerson's verse has greatly weakened whatever confidence I may ever have had in the critic as judge and arbiter. I find myself agreeing with what John Dewey said long ago in *Art as Experience*: "If judicial critics do not learn modesty from the past they pro-

---

[1] In a letter dated August 19, 1867, Browning asked his correspondent, "Did you see Emerson's new poems? with very fine and true things,—but not in any new key,—the old voice and tone." *Letters of Robert Browning, Collected by Thomas J. Wise*, Thurman L. Hood, ed., New Haven, Yale University Press, 1933, p. 119.

fess to esteem, it is not from lack of material. Their history
is largely the record of egregious blunders."[2] The critic-
as-judge knows the law and applies it to the specific case
before him. Not to know the law, or to doubt its authority,
presumably disqualifies a judge. What follows will therefore bear as little resemblance to traditional judicial criticism as I can manage without giving up the aim of trying
to get Emerson's verse read again freshly, with neither Victorian nor New Critical assumptions controlling the
reading.

But of course one never approaches any experience, literary or other, with no assumptions. I suggest that two
ideas already touched upon in my opening chapter might
be helpful in arriving at a fresh impression of the collected
poems. The first is that we read them thinking not primarily
of traditional poetic genres or time-honored poetic conventions, prosodic or other, but of what has happened since in
American poetry; the second, that we think of Emerson's
most characteristic poems—as both "Bacchus" and "Woodnotes" are, for example, but "Concord Hymn" is not, though
it is a good poem—that we think of his most characteristic
work as deeply influenced by and, in its special way, continuing the Ancient, Medieval, and Renaissance literary and
philosophic tradition of paradoxy, a way of thinking and
writing chiefly associated with prose, though it found its
way into Renaissance verse too.[3]

By the first suggestion I do not mean that we should
judge Emerson's poems simply as foreshadowing what was
to come later, as, in effect, Whitman did in his most severe
judgment of Emerson as the initial discoverer of the land
it remained for Whitman to explore.[4] Rather, I mean that

[2] Original publication date, 1934. I have quoted from the 1958
Capricorn Books reprint, p. 301.

[3] See Colie, *Paradoxia Epidemica*.

[4] Whitman's essay on Emerson in *Specimen Days and Collect*, in
which he expresses his very natural resentment at being relegated by
many to the status of a mere follower or disciple of the world-famous

we should try to allow our expectations about what is "permissible" in verse, or, in more contemporary terms, about what will "work" in a given context, to reflect our having read and responded to the work of the greatest poets who followed Emerson, particularly those who through direct influence or through the mediation of Whitman followed in the tradition he established. What I mean by the second suggestion, relating Emerson to the tradition of paradoxy, I shall try to make clear later, but first a few more remarks on what I mean by suggesting that we read Emerson's poems in what might be called a "future-oriented" frame of mind while still avoiding judging him only as a precursor.

It is perfectly true that Emerson's most important and characteristic poems may be thought of as "Americanizing" and "revising" the British Romantic tradition best exemplified for him in the poetry of Wordsworth and given its theoretical justification in the prose of Coleridge. But if his poems thus represent a "continuation," like any really significant artistic continuation they also mark a break. In only a couple of poems, chiefly in the immature "Good-bye" and in the too seldom read "Blight," does Emerson write like, sound like, or even really think like Wordsworth—though of course he very often treats what we have come to think of as Wordsworthian themes, and the older poet was crucial to Emerson's own self-discovery as a poet. (*How* crucial is often most clear when Emerson is expressing his disappointments in the older poet and his poetry.) To a reader for whom Wordsworth's work represents the culmination

---

Emerson, in effect defines Emerson's achievement as the discovery of a land left for Whitman to explore and map. Many of Whitman's detractions in the essay still seem acute, but he unfairly minimizes the extent of Emerson's own explorations in most of the areas Whitman mapped, except of course that of sex. The essay is conveniently available in Edmund Wilson's *The Shock of Recognition*. Significantly, Whitman omitted the essay from the 1887 edition of the book, preferring to let the tributes occasioned by his memories of his last visit to Emerson in 1881 stand unqualified.

of a Romantic development with a long history before it,
Emerson may seem to be a late minor follower who trans-
planted and up-dated, and in the process attenuated, the
work of the master.

But presumably most of us have not stopped responding
to poetry, including Romantic poetry, with the poetry of
Wordsworth. Another century begins to move toward its
close, and many great later poets have given us pleasure
and enlarged the world our imagination inhabits, conspicuous among them poets who would almost certainly have
written very differently if Emerson had not lived and written as he did. Knowing and having been affected by their
work, we may see Emerson's poetry as more of a beginning
—at least for us—than an end, as an opening up of possibilities, a breaking of conventions that had to be broken—and
then sometimes rediscovered—before the modern imagination could find adequate expression in verse form. The
"conventions" I am thinking of were at once conventions of
thought and conventions governing the expression of
thought in verse, habitual ways of imagining and feeling,
and habitual ways of poetic saying. Though he could write
well in several styles—of which more later—Emerson in his
most characteristic verse mixed conventional forms of accentual-syllabic prosody with seeming arbitrariness, sometimes abandoned altogether the accentual-syllabic tradition
that had been dominant since Chaucer, took unusual liberties with his rhymes, used traditional verse forms for untra-
ditional purposes, rediscovered the long-buried dipodic
tradition with its two-stress lines and indeterminate number of syllables, and very frequently turned away from logical or narrative modes of development toward the improvisational forms Whitman exploited and later poets have often
preferred. In these and other formal ways he freed the
modern imagination to express itself in verse. Freeing it, he
was also shaping it, shaping it even when he was challeng-
ing it to avoid his "errors," his failures, as, in different ways,

he did for both Emily Dickinson and Robert Frost. Whitman obviously, Pound and Williams less obviously and
more complexly but no less truly, should be numbered
among Emerson's poetic heirs, and their heirs are legion
today.

"Opening up," "freeing": for better or worse, obviously.
"Found poetry" and the undisciplined "confessional" poem
can as easily be traced to Emerson's theory and practice as
can important aspects of the later poetry of Hart Crane and
Roethke and both the formal and the thematic aspects of
the work of A. R. Ammons. "Freedom" and "license" used
to be contrasted, but now that the poet is "licensed" to do
whatever he can get away with, whatever will "work" as we
say, "license" begins to sound archaic. Perhaps we should
say that freedom may be aped by those who have nothing
worthwhile to express and so have no need for freedom.
"Free verse is like playing tennis with the net down." Still,
when Stuart Sherman noted in 1921 that Emerson's poetry
had anticipated much that was happening in the poetic
renaissance then in full flower,[5] he performed an act of
critical judgment that affords a better starting point for an
evaluation of Emerson's achievement in verse than most
later critics have. Certainly those critics who in the twenties
and even later continued to rehearse the list of Emerson's
"faults"—that is, his departures from traditional, and particularly Victorian, practice—and those still later critics like
Matthiessen who discarded the pre-modern standard for
a Modernist, "New Critical" one and found quite different,
but equally crippling, faults seem less helpful today.
"Faults" Emerson's verse has of course, lots of them and ter-

---

[5] Sherman's comments on Emerson's anticipations of the new poetry
of the day were made in the Introduction to his edition of the *Essays
and Poems of Emerson*, where he says (p. xxxix), "It is not yet adequately recognized to what extent Emerson anticipated not only
Whitman but also the poets of the present hour. He anticipates their
desire to strike up for the new world a new tune."

rible ones sometimes, by *any* normative standard, Victorian,
"New Critical," Impressionist, or, most damningly perhaps,
the standard implied by the ideals he announced in "The
Poet" and elsewhere. But so has the work of any poet who
writes very much and tries to be more than an imitator. But
what they are, and what his peculiar strength as a poet is,
must be redefined for a period almost as clearly post-Mod-
ernist as it is post-Victorian.

For a full clarification of my second suggestion, that we
think of Emerson's most characteristic poems as belonging
in the tradition of paradox, I can only refer the reader once
again to Rosalie Colie's wise and definitive study of the tradition, *Paradoxia Epidemica: The Renaissance Tradition
of Paradox.* As I see it, it is no accident that among the writers given principal emphasis in the book are several who
were extremely important to Emerson in his process of self-
discovery. Plato was for him "the" philosopher, the only
philosopher in fact who really mattered deeply to him. In
the essay on him in *Representative Men* Emerson praises
him in terms surprisingly consistent with Miss Colie's description of the paradoxical aspects of the *Parmenides*:

> They [paradoxes] play with rational discourse . . . and in
> this respect might be called anti-rational. The most famous
> such document in paradoxical anti-rationalism is surely the
> *Parmenides*, the dialogue in which opposites, contradictory
> opinions, and self-contradictions are exploited almost past
> bearing. The *Parmenides* became, during a long stage in its
> complicated history, a document in the history of mysticism,
> but it is in its construction . . . entirely rationalistic. . . .[6]

As Plato represented philosophy for Emerson, so Montaigne, that master of what Emerson in his essay on him
calls "the game of thought," represented skepticism, which
has the negative but indispensable virtue of making clear
the limitations of the understanding, the inability of rational

[6] *Paradoxia Epidemica*, pp. 7-8.

discourse and systematic philosophy to solve the riddles of
"Infinite and Finite; Relative and Absolute; Apparent and
Real...."[7]

And not only these two favorites, Plato and Montaigne,
but Sir Thomas Browne and many of the other writers who
meant the most to Emerson, including Spenser, Shakes-
speare, Milton, and George Herbert and the other Metaphysical poets, sometimes practiced the art of paradox,
which, as Colie makes clear, has among its chief aims the
use of reason (in the contemporary sense of the word, not
Coleridge's) to reduce men to wonder and tends to flourish
in periods characterized by competing value-systems and
systems of thought, in short, in periods like the Renaissance
and Emerson's own as he saw it. It was in the tradition of
paradox, particularly as the neo-Platonic practitioners of
"negative theology" availed themselves of it, that Emerson
found even his favorite symbol of both God and Reality,
eternity and infinity, the circle whose center is everywhere
and circumference nowhere.

It is not hard to understand why this clergyman without
a pulpit who had lost the received faith but remained a
very religious man, though he saw himself as in conflict
with all the orthodoxies of his age, should find himself
drawn to a paradoxical way of writing. If Trinitarian doctrines rested on "superstition" but rationalistic Unitarianism
seemed composed only of "pale negations"; if to the illuminated eye the perception of Unity was the ultimate wisdom
but the burgeoning sciences demanded and deserved respect for the news they brought of particulars; if one lived
in an age renowned for its technological "works" but felt
that the only real wealth lay in fleeting realizations of the
limitless depth of the moments of time offered by our
"days"[8]—if these were among the primary intuitions of a
son of the Puritans, what more natural than that he should

[7] "Plato," in *Representative Men, Works,* IV, pp. 143-144.
[8] "Works and Days," in *Society and Solitude, Works,* VII.

make it a lifelong occupation to use his rational intelligence to undermine the mere "understanding," and thus at once to reawaken the possibility of wonder and to promote faith, as so many of his mentors had done before him? That self-reliance should upon examination turn out to be God-reliance, resting ultimately upon self-abandonment; that the intellect thinks best when it abandons the effort to direct its thoughts; that the one Reality, the "world-soul," is both the doubter and the doubt; that God remains a circle even though neither the circle's center nor its circumference is anywhere to be found—these are some of Emerson's favorite and central paradoxes and I suggest that they and others like them will be found informing much of his best and most characteristic poetry, in his verse and in his prose.

Needless to say, just as not all of Emerson's essays are like "Self-Reliance," "Intellect," "The Over-Soul," "Circles," and "Works and Days" in moving toward prose-poetry and relying heavily on paradox, so not all of his verse is vatic in character and intention, and not all of his vatic poetry is notably paradoxical. My second suggestion for a fresh reading of Emerson as a poet in verse and prose then is a limited and qualified one; in effect, no more than that if we keep the tradition of paradoxy in mind as we read Emerson we shall be in a better position to understand and judge his achievement in his most characteristic work, including not only what we may decide is his best but also much that fails to speak to our condition, to impress us, that may even strike us as either pointless or absurd. As I said earlier and as Colie has made abundantly clear, paradox is at once a very effective and a very fragile literary form, dependent for its success not only on its author's correctly identifying what will seem to be common sense reasonableness to his contemporary readers but also on historical changes in "common sense" that, because he cannot foresee them, are quite beyond the writer's control. When Emerson's paradoxes seem most pointless or absurd to us, it is generally, it seems to me, as I have already suggested, because we no longer assume what the contemporaries he was addressing assumed. There is no point in contradicting a common-sense view that no thoughtful person holds any longer.

One of the very few judgments on which there has been widespread agreement among readers of Emerson's poems is that they are exceptionally uneven in quality. Admirers and detractors alike tend to agree on this judgment even while they interpret it differently. My own experience of reading straight through the volume of collected poems several times has shown me no reason to challenge the general opinion. There are more than a dozen poems I find myself wishing to return to frequently and think it might be possible to defend as classics of their kind, perhaps twice as many more that seem to me well worth remembering and now and then rereading despite their flaws, a larger number that I value only for a passage or two or even a line, and then the rest, the ones that do not speak to me at all, that I find boring or even irritating to read. Emerson's collected poetry is a volume to skip around in, make one's own anthology out of. Though something like this is no doubt true of the collected works of all poets except perhaps the very greatest, it seems more true of Emerson's work than it does generally of poets who put more emphasis on craft and relied less on inspiration. Distinguished poetic reputations have often rested on a smaller number of memorable poems, but perhaps few if any classic poets have published so much verse that strikes one as skirting the edge of doggerel.

No doubt there are many reasons why the bulk of Emerson's poems fail to please us, including, of course, what may appear to be the relative lack of compositional skill that went into the fashioning of them. But one thing is clear: "compositional skill" must not be interpreted as capable of being determined by the degree to which the poem in question approaches traditional prosodic regularity and logical tightness of structure, for prosodic irregularity and structural looseness are generally as prominent features of some of the poems that impress us most—"Merlin," for example —as they are of many of those that impress us least—"May-Day," for example. But even if we rule out the conventions of traditional prosody, stanzaic or structural regularity, and logical development as yardsticks by which to measure the relative success of Emerson's poems, there still remain I am sure several approaches that would avoid relying on any simplistic notion of the "rules" of good versifying and yet prove enlightening. If this essay has the effect of getting Emerson's poetry read again, others will I hope pursue such approaches.

As for myself, I should like to follow the lead provided by Emerson himself when he opened his first collection with that bafflingly paradoxical poem called "The Sphinx," a work that proved so puzzling and unpopular with his contemporaries that Edward Emerson, wanting his father to put his best foot forward, removed it to a less prominent position in the *Collected Poems* and put a more traditional and easily understood poem, "Good-bye," in its place. But I think we should assume that Emerson wanted the poem read first because it announced his own conception of his chosen role as a poet. The Sphinx was a mystery and a marvel, exciting wonder and raising unanswerable questions, riddles in fact. Edward Emerson tells us in his notes that in 1838 Emerson wrote in his Journal, "The Egyptian Sphinxes are observed to have all a countenance expressive of complacency and tranquility: an expression of health. There is much history in that fact." The same note quotes an entry in an 1859 Notebook as reading,

> I have often been asked the meaning of the "Sphinx." It is this,—The perception of identity unites all things and explains one by another, and the most rare and strange is equally facile as the most common. But if the mind live only in particulars, and see only differences (wanting the power to see the whole—all in each), then the world ad-

dresses to this mind a question it cannot answer, and each
new fact tears it in pieces, and it is vanquished by the dis-
tracting variety.[9]

Reading these two statements and the poem itself while
assuming that Emerson placed the poem as he did to give
his readers a clue to his own understanding of his chief role
as a poet brings us back to the ideas of the poet as *Dichter*
and *vates* already discussed. If Emerson really knew what
he was doing when he gave "The Sphinx" initial prominence
in *Poems*, he must have conceived of himself as assuming
the vatic role of the poet, but not "vatic" in the sense of
"moralistic," vatic rather in the riddling sense that the
words of the *vates* could be understood only by those at-
tuned to their peculiar mystery. The classic *vates* did not
give common-sense answers to practical or common-sense
questions. The *vates*, like the Sphinx, spoke in riddles, in
paradoxes. If its words contained, for those who could understand them, the answers to questions about "The fate of
the man-child, / The meaning of man," they revealed them
only in baffling paradoxes like those that conclude the
poem's second stanza:

> "Out of sleeping a waking,
> 　　Out of waking a sleep;
> Life death overtaking;
> 　　Deep underneath deep?"

These and other paradoxes would be understood by the
prepared mind as requiring still another intellectual and
spiritual paradox of him who would attain wisdom: "To vision profounder, / Man's spirit must dive." One normally
thinks of "ascending" or "rising" to vision. "Diving" for it is
precisely what Emerson undertakes in "Bacchus" and, less
successfully, in other poems that make room in the imagination for night, chaos, and "the old despair." Only a paradoxical vision can persuade us that "Love works at the cen-

[9] *Poems*, p. 412.

tre," in the One, despite the confusing deceptions of all the "particulars," the "differences," exhibited by the Many.

Taking "The Sphinx" as a clue to both intention and method, then, I should like to examine a number of Emerson's poems, starting with several that do not greatly impress me and ending with several that do. All of them are vatic poems in intention and all of them exploit paradoxes. The chief difference, as I read them, between the relatively unimpressive and the impressive poems is that in the unimpressive ones the paradoxes do not "work," for a variety of reasons. There are, I repeat, other, quite different reasons for the failure of many of Emerson's weaker poems, but I want to delay consideration of the various poetic problems he found it difficult to solve in verse for later consideration, where a discussion of some of his difficulties may help to explain why much of his best "poetry" is to be found in his essays rather than in his poems.

An examination of the characteristics of three "middling" poems that are typical of Emerson's verse both formally and philosophically may offer a way of beginning to understand his unevenness and the widely divergent evaluations readers of his verse have expressed over the years. "World-Soul," "Destiny," and "The Humble-Bee," which he placed prominently early in *Poems*, are written in forms he very often chose, the "Short Meter" of the hymns, three-stress quatrains rhyming a-b-c-b; four-stress lines intermingled with shorter ones, rhyming irregularly in quatrains, couplets, and triplets; and four-stress couplets regular enough, for the most part, to be described as tetrameter. All three poems treat ideas central to his thinking, the underpinning of his faith. All three may be read as nineteenth-century versions of the "negative theology" beloved of the neo-Platonic mystics, and all three rely on paradox, on negating the seemingly obvious and thus, insofar as they succeed, shocking us into a "vision profounder."

Though Emerson sometimes seems to distinguish between "World-Soul" and "Over-Soul" (which is not itself one of the circles of experience but the "eternal generator" of them), the poem he entitled "World-Soul" seems to me not to make the distinction, contenting itself with contrasting the Many with the One, the infinite Mind or Spirit to which our finite minds have access and of which they and the world are a part. If "self-reliance" is to be justified as other than selfishness or idiosyncrasy, there must be a "World-Soul" to make it possible to say that "self-reliance" is really "God-reliance," and the nature and ways of the World-Soul must be understood so far as possible. But common-sense reason provides no better access to such understanding than "superstitious" Trinitarian dogma. The poem condenses some of the paradoxical ideas expounded in the essay "The Over-Soul" and thus implies the rationale of Emerson's central ideas about the conduct of life. "Destiny" treats an aspect of the same subject, putting the emphasis on the paradoxical nature of our relationship to the World-Soul. The key to self-reliance, the poem makes clear, is, paradoxically, self-forgetfulness; power comes only through submission to one's destiny. The poem contains new versions of several paradoxes that were very familiar to Emerson's orthodox ancestors: one must lose his life in order to save it, and only Grace, over which we have no control, not our own Works, can "justify" us in the end. The fatalistic and quietistic strands in Emerson's thought have a prominent place in the poem.

"The Humble-Bee" is at once a less ambitious and, I think, a more successful poem. "Nature" for Emerson was a word so freighted with sacred significance that he never repeated his early attempt at logical discursive definition of its several meanings. In the poem he attempts to evoke a sense of the awe and wonder Nature inspired in him by combining description of a common insect with paradoxical statements prompted by observation of the insect's activities. The form of the poem is consistent with, even in a sense may be said to exemplify, the ideas about Nature he had expressed in his early manifesto. There Nature had been de-

fined as at once fact and symbol, matter and spirit, discipline and the possibility of transcendence. The poem takes
off from the imaginative flight of *Nature's* final chapter,
"Spirit," where we learn that "As a plant upon the earth, so
a man rests upon the bosom of God; he is nourished by un-
failing fountains, and draws at his need inexhaustible power. . . . Once inhale the upper air, being admitted to behold
the absolute natures of justice and truth, and we learn that
man has access to the entire mind of the Creator, is himself
the creator in the finite."[10] This is Emerson's version of the
Beatific Vision.

The "inexhaustible power" and the realization of our one-
ness with the divine are to be achieved, the poem tells us,
by methods more akin to worship than to study. Beatitude
it seems is not to be seized but to be prepared for and
awaited, as Emerson's ministerial ancestors had thought the
reception of Grace must be. The wisdom of the world is
mocked by it, all our cunning useless in our attempt to
achieve what it offers. To put the same matter in less theological terms, the poem belongs in that paradoxical tradition of which perhaps Erasmus' *The Praise of Folly* is the
most famous example. The paternal—the "reasonable"—aspects of Nature as commodity, language, and discipline—
fact, idea, authority—are left behind in the poem's celebration of the unreasonable maternal. "Mother Nature" is our
matrix, "a situation or surrounding substance within which
something originates, develops, or is contained," as one dictionary puts it. For the poem, and for Emerson, the final
"or" of the definition just quoted should be an "and."
Though Emerson never admitted to full-fledged pantheism,
he thought it useless to try to separate the intermingled
realities of Nature, Man, and God. "The Humble-Bee" expresses in paradoxes a joyous religious submission to the
Great Mother who bore us and still contains us.

I have called all three poems "middling," which may

[10] *Works*, I, p. 68.

mean no more than that I find it impossible to respond to
them without reservations. The hymnal background of the
verse form of "The World-Soul" seems appropriate enough
for a poem that is in effect a Transcendental psalm, a religious song of praise. (The Transcendental vision had no
use for other kinds of psalms, especially for those of lament
or petition.) As the psalmist of Psalm 19 had been thankful
for the way in which "The heavens declare the glory of
God, the vault of heaven declares his handiwork,"[11] particularly in the rising of the sun, so Emerson opens his poem
with "Thanks to the morning light" for its reminder of the
"eternal rings" woven by the stars in the heavens. Then, still
in his first stanza, he gives thanks for those persons around
him who sometimes also serve as symbolic pointers to the
nature and ways of the World-Soul,

> Thanks to each man of courage,
> To the maids of holy mind,
> To the boy with his games undaunted
> Who never looks behind—

a theme restated in the fourth stanza's lines about the an-
gelic figure in the parlor, stranger or friend, who suddenly
recalls him to the certainty of Transcendental Truth even
in a world where we find that "Trade and the streets en-
snare us, / Our bodies are weak and worn."

Yet the poem's final ringing affirmations strike me as too
easy, unfounded, even sentimental, as no Biblical psalm that
I recall ever does. Perhaps part of the reason is that though
both the poem and Psalm 19 contrast the glory of God with
the general unrighteousness of man, Emerson explicitly locates wickedness exclusively in society in general, particularly society in cities, while the psalmist locates it in man
and his ways, including the psalmist's own—"But who can
detect his own failings? / . . . from pride preserve your
servant." Both psalm and poem assert that the ways of the

---

[11] The translation is that of the English version of *The Jerusalem
Bible*.

Most High are not our ways, that they upset our limited notions of right and wrong ("The Law of Yahweh is perfect,"
our own laws most imperfect), but there the resemblance
ends, for what the speaker in the poems calls "Destiny"
seems today more like a Darwinian description of evolution
with its "survival of the fittest" than like a series of religious
paradoxes:

> He serveth the servant,
>   The brave he loves amain;
> He kills the cripple and the sick,
>   And straight begins again;
> For gods delight in gods,
>   And thrust the weak aside;
> To him who scorns their charities
>   Their arms fly open wide.

This may well be the way things go in the world, I find myself reflecting, but what is there in the spectacle to prompt
religious awe? The lines that immediately follow, in the
next stanza, promising "The fairer world" in some future
time to come seem more like a retreat on Emerson's part
from his own paradoxes than like a development of them.
They seem to me to leave us still having to know chiefly
from outside the poem that, since Emerson took over without much change the ethical side of his religious heritage,
the lines must be intended as paradoxes. Certainly we must
assume it gave him no pleasure to watch the killing of crip-
ples and the sick. It was not *his* will but Destiny's that was
being, and would always be, done, and that he must somehow not just accept but find meaningful:

> The patient Daemon sits,
> With roses and a shroud;
> He has his way, and deals his gifts, —
> But ours is not allowed.

At any rate, probably for a variety of reasons, those parts
of the poem that describe what's wrong with society ("the
System") seem to me to come through much more strongly

than the final affirmations. Though the second stanza, describing the "cities of proud hotels" where "vice nestles" in the chambers, has an archaic and hollow ring somehow even to those well acquainted with "crime on the streets," it ends with lines we are not likely to find fault with: "And the light-outspeeding telegraph / Bears nothing on its beam." It is not hard to agree that our "politics are base" and our "letters do not cheer," though the lines are too abstract to strike us with much power, and it may even be generally true that "We plot and corrupt each other." But what unstated convictions, we should like to know, support the analogy drawn in the last stanza between nature's seasonal renewal and man's? Why is April *not* "the cruelest month"?

> Spring still makes spring in the mind
>   When sixty years are told;
> Love wakes anew this throbbing heart,
>   And we are never old.
> Over the winter glaciers
>   I see the summer glow,
> And through the wild-piled snowdrift,
>   The warm rosebuds below.

If the poem has persuaded us, we should find ourselves in the mood of the speaker, confident that glimpses of Nature's beautiful order and the inspiration afforded by exceptional people are sufficient to permit us not only to accept the ways of the World-Soul but to transcend time and the terrors of history. But I suspect that the ending of the poem, with its clichés ("throbbing heart") and its impossible-to-imagine key image (roses do *not* bloom beneath snowdrifts), will find most modern readers as unpersuaded as ever.

"World-Soul" in short seems to me to contain some fine lines and a number of strong images but finally to affirm a faith that appears unfounded and thus sentimental. Emerson believed of course that the best poetry is always affirmative, once summing up the matter in the simple equation "poetry is faith."[12] But since a poem is something made as well as something said, the mere assertion of a faith is not enough, at least for anyone but the body of believers who already hold it and enjoy hearing it repeated. One of the reasons why Emerson was often a better poet in his prose than in his verse is illustrated by a comparison of his final affirmation in "The World-Soul" with the affirmative ending of the essay "Experience," where, after looking closely at all those aspects of life that make it seem dream-like and destructive of any certainty or any ideal meaning, he concludes that the truths of the outward life do not cancel the intuitions of the heart, which tell us to have courage, "never mind the defeat," and believe that "victory" and "true romance" are still possible. The essay's final paradoxical affirmation has been earned by a long look at the hard facts; the poem's strikes us as just asserted, after a very incomplete look at just some of the facts. To read it as a poem that paradoxically affirms religious faith by negating the consolations of traditional faith (God loves the poor, etc.), we have to think our way back into a frame of mind and a historical situation that were Emerson's but are not ours.

Emerson's fondness for early seventeenth-century poets like George Herbert has led a number of critics to describe his poetry as influenced by the example of the Metaphysicals, but if the final image of roses budding beneath the snow in "The World-Soul" is a Metaphysical paradox, it seems so only in Samuel Johnson's sense of "farfetched." Emily Dickinson echoed the theme of the poem's ending in several better poems, particularly in "An altered look upon the hills," but she also countered it a number of times, as in her great "In snow thou comest" and "A light exists in Spring," in which she sees that "It passes and we stay." "The World-Soul," I conclude, is a very characteristic middling Emerson poem. So far as I can tell from an examination of my own response, the chief reason why I find it only mid-

[12] "Poetry and Imagination," in *Letters and Social Aims, Works,* VIII, p. 35.

dling is that I tend to read its paradoxes as statements of obvious facts. If so, it would not be the first instance of what was meant as paradox coming to seem literal truth.[13]

"Destiny" develops a part of the theme of "The World-Soul"—that the Lord's ways are not our ways—but comparing it with the Psalms is less revealing, for "Destiny" is not a hymn of praise and thanksgiving but a wisdom poem, admonitory and even didactic in tone. Yet "didactic" is hardly the right word, for the poem offers no practical instructions or exhortations, it merely says in effect, this is the way things are, these are the characteristics of that "Destiny" which in "The World-Soul" had been identified as the visible manifestation of the One working among the Many in history. The speaker here understands and accepts the ways of Destiny and addresses himself in the opening lines to those who have not yet achieved wisdom, to all the "you's" in the world:

> That you are fair or wise is vain,
> Or strong, or rich, or generous;
> You must add the untaught strain
> That sheds beauty on the rose.

Of the several paradoxes here, the most shocking is the last one: what we are told we "must" add is of course not at all within our power to add. So much for logic! As for piety, since we have been thinking of the Psalms, one more comparison may not be inappropriate: adding an "untaught," and therefore presumably given, not learned,

13 Compare, for example, what Colie has to say about Gorgias' originally paradoxical praise of Helen of Troy: "Sometimes a paradox fails to work as a paradox, to surprise or to dazzle by its incongruities. Gorgias' praise of Helen is a pretty example of such failure: originally a mock-encomium of the woman who was 'obviously' unworthy of conventional praise, . . . Gorgias' oration was so effective that Helen became, not a paradoxical, but a proper subject for encomium, a source of many set-pieces on the most beautiful woman in the world. In this case, paradox became orthodox." *Paradoxia Epidemica*, p. 8.

"strain" is a rough equivalent of the Psalmist's assumption of Yahweh's special concern for his Chosen People, a paradoxical concern that the people had neither learned nor earned, could only give thanks for, or petition for further signs of. But if there is thus a kind of religious equivalence to be noted, there is also a crucial difference between any of Emerson's poems, this one especially, and any of the Psalms. The Psalms are religious songs for use in public worship by a body of believers, addressed at once to those believers and to Yahweh, with no need to explain or defend the faith they spring from and give expression to. Emerson's faith is his own, and he must make it moving if not acceptable to us his readers, make us at least suspend our disbelief, if his poem is to compel the assent he hopes for. If "poetry is faith," as he said, the Psalms can survive—survive both as religion and as poetry—the application even of what probably strikes us as an unnecessarily restrictive definition; but when we apply the definition to Emerson's own poems of faith the burden it places on them very often seems too great for them to bear, except perhaps to whatever "disciples" he may still have. With his faith as he held it no longer available to us, the poems must bear the enormous burden of making it seem at once credible and attractive, prompting us to say *Amen*, "So be it," at the end. Only a few of them seem to me to succeed. The majority of his strongest poems note the cost of the true vision, the "withering" self-knowledge that fell on Uriel, remind us of our failures to achieve it ("Days"), or humble us with the Earth-Mother's laughter ("Hamatreya")—in short, give expression both to the faith of the "voyager of light and noon" and to the realism of the shrewd observer in this divided "Plotinus-Montaigne" of a poet.

But to return to "Destiny." I might as well confess at once that I don't like the poem very much, but as far as I can tell my failure to respond to it favorably has little or nothing to do with its *formal* qualities as verse. It does not bother me that its generally four-stress lines often demand considera-

ble forcing to be read as iambic tetrameter, or that they are
sometimes replaced by dimeters or trimeters, or that the
rhyming is highly irregular, varying from the initial quatrain to couplets and triplets and disappearing entirely in
places. The prosodic irregularities seem to me in fact to
function as examples of "metre-making argument," with the
unexpected short lines serving to throw special emphasis
precisely where the sense of the poem says it should come,
as in the dipodics "And another is born" and "Under his
tongue," or, even more clearly, in the unrhymed three-stress
lines that aphoristically sum up the main thrust of the
poem's meaning:

> One thing is forever good;
> That one thing is Success.

No, it is not Emerson's faulty technique that the post-
Victorian and early modern critics of the poetry made so
much of that bothers me. It is rather that this wisdom poem
seems to me not deeply wise but only "worldly-wise" and
too well armored against grief. Some of the late poems of
Frost, for example "Provide, Provide," express the need for
this hard-boiled "wisdom" better, just because their tone
makes perfectly clear the speaker's awareness of all the implications of what he is saying, including the moral insensi-
tivity and psychic withdrawal this kind of wisdom entails.
Frost's toughness amounts to a cynicism that knows itself
to be cynicism and seems to justify itself in the poem, however much we may deplore cynicism in the abstract, when
we have turned away from the poem to meditate on disembodied moral truths. Emerson's "Destiny," by contrast,
may strike us as cynical but the speaker's tone suggests that
he sees it as wisdom, not cynicism. He is instructing us in
"the way things are" and trying to get us to approve, as he
does. "Common sense," it would seem, is all we need to
know the correct answer to his rhetorical questions. Of
what use, for example, is "the soldier's mail, / Unless he
conquer and prevail?" None, obviously.

"The World-Soul" placed a part of its emphasis on the
same observation that history does not illustrate or support
our moral ideas, but in that poem the call for the courage
that will allow us to accept the ways of an impersonal
Destiny seemed to me partially to save the poem as a kind
of wisdom even if the ending appeared sentimental. Here,
except as I remind myself that what I am reading "straight"
was probably intended as paradox aimed at the faith of
"believers," I find no wisdom at all, unless a purely pruden-
tial and callous shrewdness is counted as wisdom. It may
well be advisable for us to toughen up, harden our hearts,
if only that we may survive a little longer; but that is not
what it seems to me Emerson meant by his poem, and it is
certainly not what the great sages and religious teachers
have meant by wisdom. If we do not read such lines as the
following as *unwittingly* scrapping the whole Judeo-
Christian moral-religious heritage, how are we to read
them?

> Alas! that one is born in blight,
> Victim of perpetual slight:
> When thou lookest on his face,
> Thy heart saith, 'Brother, go thy ways!'

I find it much easier to understand the lack of concern for
the fate of those outside the small band of the Elect that
Emerson's Calvinist forebears betrayed than I do the cal-
lousness of this advice masquerading as realistic observation. Wigglesworth showed more pity in allowing the un-
baptized who died in infancy to suffer in "the *easiest* room
in Hell," contrary to doctrinal teaching, than Emerson does
here. True, our heart does say what the poem has it say all
too often. If this were all, it would merely state a fact, de-
plorable no doubt but not less true. But this is not all. What
we know of Emerson's views from outside the poem is con-
firmed within the poem: if we listen to the "melody, /
Which melts the world" of sense "into a sea," we shall be
prepared to accept and even applaud the heart's turning

away. Emerson is here—and of course often elsewhere—in effect preparing the American conscience to welcome Social Darwinism as a justifying rationalization for the competitive jungle of late nineteenth-century capitalism. It is right and proper, he says, that only the fittest survive, and that the test of their fitness should be the fact of their survival. That success is the only thing "forever good" is not only the lesson of evolution, Emerson seems to be telling us in "Destiny," it is the will and decree of Yahweh, God, the World-Soul, the One, whose ways of putting His will into effect appear to us as Destiny. How comforting to those who have succeeded to realize that their success is proof of their virtue, even of their godliness. Never perhaps were "ought" and "is" more miserably confused and confounded by a poet of any merit than they appear to be by Emerson in "Destiny." Reminding ourselves that Emerson could not have been wholly unaware of the way the poem's doctrines reduce ethics to nonsense, and so must have thought of them as instructive, as paradoxes are, does not really help much, for we know too much about men of his century less sensitive than he for whom such ideas seemed literal truths to read them paradoxically. It is hard to know whether Emerson's technique betrayed him in this poem or whether he has been betrayed by history.

I am not unaware of my beginning to sound like a less brilliant Yvor Winters, who sometimes strikes me as passing off moral indignation as literary criticism. So be it. It seems to me that the unconventional formal aspects of the poem are essential to whatever strength it has as a memorable aphoristic statement of the immense gap between the world's ways and our ideas for remaking it, between history and the ideal, between the ideals we profess and the motions of our hearts. It is very true that if we wish to stay sane, we had better admit reality as it is and not twist it to fit our own private dreaming, but if we find important aspects of reality non-moral, unjust, even absurd, are we under any obligation to call them good and give them our

blessing? There is much shrewdness in the speaker's observation concerning his reaction to others that "I care not how
you are dressed, / . . . Nor whether your name is base or
brave: / Nor for the fashion of your behavior; / But whether you charm me," but to conclude from this that satisfying
the survival instinct is the only choice open to man is to betray not only, as I have said, our Western moral heritage
but other, and very important, insights that formed a part
of Emerson's own Transcendental faith. If you charm me,
I will call you artless and God-inspired, Emerson is saying
in effect—a message I find irritating, not "inspiring."

"The Humble-Bee" strikes me as a much better poem,
though still likely to seem a "middling" one to most contemporary readers. Nineteenth-century readers were conditioned to respond to the poem's paradoxical praise of nature at the expense of culture, particularly, by mid-century,
to its praise of those "humbler" aspects of nature than the
"picturesque" crags and waterfalls that had delighted and
instructed an earlier generation. In choosing a common and
not particularly beautiful or remarkable insect and rein-
forcing the point of his choice by using the archaic form of
the bumblebee's name to suggest a common-sense view of
the insect's place in nature before going about paradoxically upsetting that view, Emerson expressed the sensibility
of an age that would soon have the opportunity to share
Whitman's paradoxical admiration for "beetles rolling balls
of dung." It may well be that if we are going to keep the
planet habitable, we shall have to recover a sense of nature
as "sacred," but with that feeling now largely lost, much of
the emotional freight carried by the key words and con-
cepts of "The Humble-Bee" is unavailable to us. Paradox,
once again, is one of the most brittle of literary forms.

Still it is not hard to recognize, if we will open ourselves
to an attentive and receptive reading of it, that the poem is
full of precise and vivid images, the best of them highly
charged imaginatively; that its subject as described sym-
bolically condenses, renders in visual terms, Emerson's

whole outlook about the proper "conduct of life" for one
who recognizes that he is embosomed in nature, the uncon-
ditioned; and that its four-stress, predominantly trochaic
couplets that occasionally become triplets and even, once,
a quatrain offer not only a good deal of emphasis but sufficient variety. Its best lines function at once as accurate
description of the bee's habits and movements, as seen by
the human observer, and as tropes for Emerson's own ideal
self-image, revelations of the reasons for his unqualified
praise of the "humble" "Insect lover of the sun." ("Humble"
of course not in the sense of "meek," "inoffensive," or "def-
erential," but in the sense of "lowly," "unpretentious": I
think we should credit Emerson with choosing to say "humble-bee" rather than "bumblebee" because it reinforced his
meaning.) As anyone deeply affected by the tradition of
paradoxy might, Emerson placed the highest value on self-
reliance just because he knew how minute he was in relation to the All, how insignificant indeed all mankind and
even the Earth itself was in the physical cosmos being revealed by science. Knowing this, he felt his only access to
power lay in becoming a humble "lover of the sun," the un-
conditioned source of light and so of life, the perfect ana-
logue for God for an anti-rationalist paradoxist in the neo-
Platonic tradition like Emerson.

    "Sailor of the atmosphere"—the sailor ventures on the
sea, which is little known, full of risk, at once source of life
and threat of death, vast, powerful, terrible, beautiful.
Emerson wanted to be, and I think in part succeeded in becoming, such a sailor of the cosmic atmosphere. "Swimmer
through the waves of air; / Voyager of light and noon"—a
swimmer is even less sheltered from the dangers of the sea
than a sailor, who at least has a boat or ship under him for
support. A swimmer achieves survival and freedom of
movement only by daring, paradoxically, to immerse himself in what threatens to drown him. So the bee by trusting
himself to the least solid, the most imperceptible, of the
"four elements" can reach "the green silence" of the secret

places of nature and there, particularly in the vital natural process that "Turns the sod to violets," sing his "mellow, breezy bass" of praise.

But if the modern reader can admire and respond to the first half of the poem's symbolization of Emerson's own quest as a voyager searching for light and noon, he is likely to respond less positively to the last half. Here the universal seeking of the light is seen from the other side, as it were, as a flight and denial as much as a seeking. "Aught unsavory or unclean / Hath my insect never seen"—but *we* have seen much unsavoriness and uncleanness, for the distinctions involved have meaning for us, if not for bees. The bee can appear to "mock at fate and care" because, presumably lacking self-consciousness and the ability to imagine the future, he can discover nothing that threatens him or gives him any reason for "care." What seems mockery then is only unawareness. To paraphrase Melville, "Seeing only what is fair" as the bee does is equivalent to denying reality to the dark half of the world, to becoming willfully blind, in short. But to will to be oblivious of the dark is in effect to seek the dark. Perhaps only in a condition in which unconsciousness is felt to be preferable to consciousness will it seem true that the bee, Emerson's "Yellow-breeched philosopher," is "Wiser far than human seer." Beneath Emerson's gay, paradoxical celebration of trust, participation in natural process, and the kind of instinctive behavior that takes one toward the light and gives one power, there seems to exist, for the modern reader at least, a strong undercurrent flowing in the opposite direction, toward darkness and oblivion. If this is the poem's final paradox, one doubts that Emerson himself was aware of it.

As a poet who defined his role as that of Namer and Sayer, Emerson in his characteristic poems went on naming the same realities—perceivable only from his angle of vision, or only, paradoxically, by the transparent eyeball—and giving utterance to some of the same ideas in his finest poems that we have found in those poems I have called "middling." Neither a development occurring in time—a sudden "finding of himself," a radical change in his ideas, after which he wrote differently—nor a clear distinction in subject matter, theme, or style separate the best poems from the poorest. Rather, his own poems seem to illustrate the truth, for his kind of poet at least, of his belief that all true poetry is the product of inspiration. Sometimes he seems inspired, sometimes not.

To offer the presence or absence of "inspiration" as an explanation of why we find some poems good and some not is in effect not to explain but to avoid the question. We must conclude, I think, that the appearance of distinguished poems in a collection in which all his verse was presented chronologically (a volume we are still awaiting) would be, after the middle thirties, almost unpredictable. Almost, but not quite, for after 1846 there is a gradual lessening of power. Of the new poems in *May-Day and Other Pieces*, only "Brahma," "The Titmouse," "Terminus," and possibly "Days" and "The Boston Hymn" deserve comparison with the best poems in the 1847 *Poems*. "Each and All," "The Problem," "Uriel," "Hamatreya," "The Rhodora," "The Snow-Storm," "Monadnoc," "Merlin," "Bacchus," and "Threnody" are all in the earlier collection.

"Uriel," "Merlin" (both parts), "Bacchus," "Hamatreya," and "Brahma" seem to me his greatest poems. I say "greatest" rather than "best" with full awareness that for at least a generation now none of our finest critics, or at any rate our most influential critics, have thought "great" properly applicable to any of Emerson's poems. But these poems seem great to me, and I believe that future reassessments of our poetic heritage will reveal a widening circle of agreement. If not, I will not be the first critic proved mistaken.

As Emerson said, why a poem moves us deeply, exciting

our admiration, must always remain something of a mystery.[14] The best a critic can do to explain his positive evaluation is to talk around the subject, meanwhile revealing both something of himself and something of the poem, hoping that the values he finds in it will be found by some others too once he has called attention to them, hoping that his responses will be found to be not wholly idiosyncratic. I shall not attempt "close readings" even of the five poems I have just named as my choices for "greatest," for increasingly as the years go by I find an uninterrupted series of "close readings" tedious, though I have produced my share of them in the past. Instead, I shall say only what it is that seems to me most important and most impressive about these poems. As for the many other poems that impress me as distinguished, I have had something to say about several of them in *American Poets*, so I shall merely name the most important of them and invite the test of a rereading. They include "Each and All," "The Problem," "The Sphinx," "Alphonso of Castile," "Mithridates," "The Rhodora," "The Snow-Storm," "Monadnoc," the "Ode to Channing," "Blight," "Threnody," "Concord Hymn," "Boston Hymn," "Days," "The Titmouse," "Terminus," "Circles," "The Bohemian Hymn," "Grace," "Monadnoc from Afar," "Music," "Cosmos," "The Miracle," "Limits," and, among the many fine passages in "Fragments on Nature and Life," especially the ones editorially entitled "Water" and "Nahant" in the Centenary Edition.

"Uriel" certainly does not seem to me as it did to Frost "the greatest Western poem yet" but it seems so distinguished, original, and memorable a prophetic utterance that it is not at all hard to understand why, given his bias and his sympathies, Frost valued it as he did. It is a paradoxical fable that far transcends the interest attaching to its origin in the controversy over Emerson's heretical Divinity School ad-

14 "Poetry and Imagination," *passim.*

dress. The dangerous heresies of the address have long since ceased to seem threatening to most of us, but the antinomian heart of the address is still available in the poem, and still "dangerous" to every orthodoxy, religious, scientific, humanistic, or any other. Rational humanistic distinctions, gradations, subordinations, dogmas are as much threatened as Fundamentalist or Evangelical ones by the vision summarized in the poem's central paradoxes:

'Line in nature is not found;
Unit and universe are round;
In vain produced, all rays return;
Evil will bless, and ice will burn.'

The fear-reaction of the conservative old gods to the new revelation may have been excessively defensive but it was more perceptive than that of modern readers who find no challenge to their own orthodoxy, whatever it may be, in the poem. "The bounds of good and ill were rent," the old gods thought, and they were right if we understand "good" and "ill" to mean: what is commonly so called and understood to be, perhaps prematurely and inadequately understood to be, right and wrong, true and false. The poem's thrust against the notion that truth is static and *ours* and against any moralism that is not in some degree open-ended is as sharp today as it was when Emerson took this way of replying to his clerical opponents.

The four-stress couplets work beautifully for Emerson's purposes here. There is a constant interplay between the demands of the metrical pattern and the demands of the sense, in which the impact of the merely necessary lines is diminished. "To his ears was evident," for example, may be read as having the expected four stresses, but they go by very quickly. Similarly, the force of the lines containing the revelations is increased—"In vain produced, all rays return," for example—as the lines are slowed by their four strong stresses. Though the prosody of the poem is rather more regular than was common with Emerson, it is in no sense mechanical, to my ear at least. And the "liberty" Emerson takes of starting with a quatrain giving the setting of his tale, then shifting to couplets for the rest of the poem, seems appropriate, for the fable illustrates the polarities and equivalences, the returns and echoes of "Balance-loving Nature" which, as we are told in "Merlin II," "made all things in pairs," so that rhyming couplets may be thought of as echoing nature's own ways, thus embodying an important part of what the poem means. In the form of the poem, which "defies reverend use," then, as well as in the fable it relates, we have in "Uriel" a work that can survive the application of the standards implied in a somewhat cryptic passage in "Poetry and Imagination":

> In good society, nay, among the angels in heaven, is not everything spoken in fine parable, and not so servilely as it befell to the sense? All is symbolized. Facts are not foreign, as they seem, but related. Wait a little and we see the return of the remote hyperbolic curve.[15]

"Merlin" and "Bacchus," both written in the outburst of creative energy that came in 1845-1846, are central, characteristic, very strong expressions of a cluster of ideas that were very important to Emerson and that remained essentially unaltered between their first formulation in "The Poet" and their expansive and rambling restatement in "Poetry and Imagination" some thirty years later. The judgment as to which is the greater poem is likely to reflect the reader's predisposition to value strength over order or the other way around. "Merlin" with its two parts and its improvisational movement may strike some as a "rambling" poem containing a larger number of unforgettable lines, "Bacchus" as more transparently coherent—by logical standards. Together the two poems form the classic American statements in verse of the Romantic poetic ideal that much of our best and most characteristic poetry has sought

15 *Ibid.*, p. 71.

to exemplify. And they are not only the first such statements, they remain the best.

Emerson identified very strongly with Malory's Merlin as he knew him in the prose translation available to him. Increasingly conscious of his own paucity of "talent" as a poet —though perhaps he had "genius"—he was drawn to Merlin as a "bard" who could be thought of as best exemplifying the ideas that introduce the section on "Bards and Trouveurs" in "Poetry and Imagination," which begins:

> The metallic force of primitive words makes the superiority of the [poetic] remains of the rude ages. It costs the early bard little talent to chant more impressively than the later, more cultivated poets. His advantage is that his words are things. . . .
>
> I find or fancy more true poetry . . . in . . . bardic fragments . . . than in many volumes of British Classics.[16]

A little later in the essay he quotes, for several pages, the episodes of the dialogue of Gawain with Merlin, who is imprisoned—in Emerson's version, not in Malory's—in his castle of air deep in the forest, with only one human tie left, that to his true love, his mistress, the only one still able to speak to him, who had imprisoned him and yet visited him at her pleasure. (Emerson had long since given up visiting and reopening Ellen's tomb by this time, but she still held the only key to his heart.) Magician paradoxically powerless to effect his own release from a paradoxical prison without bars, prophet, lost to those who loved and sought him, Merlin the bard awakened the deepest responses in Emerson's imagination, as his treatment of him in the essay makes very clear.[17] The depth of his response may be judged, more in-

---

[16] *Ibid.*, pp. 58-59.

[17] A still useful discussion of what Emerson knew—and did not know—about the "Bardic" tradition in general and Merlin considered as a bard in particular is contained in Nelson F. Adkins, "Emerson and the Bardic Tradition," *PMLA*, 63 (1948), 662-677. In summary, most of what Emerson knew he got at second or third hand from

directly, from the imaginative strength of the poem to which Merlin's name gives the title.

I have emphasized Emerson's discussion of the mystic Merlin in his late essay because it seems to me to open up an aspect of the poem that has received too little attention. True, the Merlin of the poem is a "kingly bard" whose words are "Artful thunder" and so akin to the messages of Jove and Yahweh, who also spoke in the thunder. When he strikes the chords of his instrument his mere words become "blows [that] are strokes of fate" powerful enough to "modulate the king's affairs." Yet the price he must pay for the power that results from his penetrating and conveying the "Secrets of the solar track" is a very high one: in effect, paradoxically, giving up control of his own destiny, yielding himself to the fates that only he can interpret. The ending of "Merlin II," almost never quoted or cited, is crucial. It is "Nemesis," fate, that "finishes the song," with the poet serving as interpreter:

> Subtle rhymes, with ruin rife,
> Murmur in the house of life,
> Sung by the Sisters as they spin;
> In perfect time and measure they
> Build and unbuild our echoing clay.
> As the two twilights of the day
> Fold us music-drunken in.

Poetry thus conceived is quite literally a "matter of life and death," too important obviously to be heard in the "jin-

---

such sources as Blair's *Rhetoric*, which he had been required to study in college. "It is doubtful," the author concludes, "whether Emerson was well informed regarding bardic literature when in 1845 and 1846 he wrote 'Merlin.'" I suspect that a similarly careful investigation of his sources would show that Emerson was seldom truly "well informed" about any of the subjects he wrote best about. With "Hamatreya" as the only conspicuous exception that comes to mind, the "information" he needed came from the work his imagination did as it played over a few facts, or supposed facts, such as that Merlin's magic gave him power, his imprisonment isolated him and rendered him powerless, and his prophecies proved to be true.

gling serenader's art" or in the "tinkle of piano strings."
Paradoxically intertwined life and death, prophecies uttered by prisoners, life promised only because death is seen
and accepted—all these paradoxes seem to me to be stated
or implied in the poem. But as Rosalie Colie noted in *Paradoxia Epidemica*, successful paradox cannot be paraphrased.[18] Still, it should be clear that interpretations of the
poem which note only that it rejects "talented" poetry in
favor of inspired prophetic poetry are quite insufficient.

Just a word on the poem's verse form. It strikes me as one
of Emerson's closest approaches to achieving his own announced ideal of organic or functional form, "metre-making
argument." The poem begins with a stanza of Common
Meter,

> Thy trivial harp will never please
> Or fill my craving ear;
> Its chords should ring as blows the breeze,
> Free, peremptory, clear, —

then moves into irregular three or four stress quatrains for
the rest of the first section. Its most famous lines must be
described as irregularly rhymed "free verse" not unlike the
verse that opens Eliot's "Prufrock":

> Great is the art,
> Great be the manners, of the bard.
> He shall not his brain encumber
> With the coil of rhythm and number;
> But, leaving rule and pale forethought,
> He shall aye climb
> For his rhyme.
> 'Pass in, pass in,' the angels say,
> 'In to the upper doors,
> Nor count compartments of the floors,
> But mount to paradise
> By the stairway of surprise.'

The rest of the poem is written with only slightly greater
regularity, with the stresses varying from two to five and

18 *Paradoxia Epidemica*, p. 35.

the rhymes sometimes making couplets, sometimes triplets, sometimes quatrains—and sometimes simply disappearing. But—and this of course is a judgment each reader must check for himself—the poem made from all these irregular pieces does not seem "formless"; its movement does not seem arbitrary but inevitable. I suspect that few poets capable of really understanding the poem would want to try to improve its form.

The call for a poetry possessing the power of inspired prophecy because it is produced by a poet who has recognized and submitted to the skeins woven by the fatal sisters, and so is enabled to find the words to give voice to life's own "subtle rhymes," is subordinated in "Merlin" to the poem's presentation of its more overt subjects. Those subjects are of course the contrast between conventional poesy and true prophetic poetry in both manner and effect; the true poet's way of working, or, when inspiration fails, of keeping silent (as Emerson would put this later in "Poetry and Imagination," ". . . either inspiration or silence. . . . Much that we call poetry is but polite verse.");[19] and the relation of the poet's rhymes to the "rhymes" of nature, a relationship that explains the source of the poet's power. That such poetry would be Dionysian, not Apollonian, and paradoxical, not logical, is clear enough, as I have tried to suggest, but it is not emphasized, is not at the center of the poem's attention. The poem's central paradox is the familiar one, that only artlessness can produce the greatest art.

In "Bacchus" the call for a kind of poetry not simply paradoxical but ecstatic, even "drunken," or perhaps better said, for the kind of poetry that only a drunken poet skilled in paradoxy could produce, is closer to the center of the poem, though the explicit subject is the poet's prayer for the kind of consciousness necessary for the production of such poetry. "The kind of consciousness": better, perhaps, the escape from the conscious control of "reasonableness" that

19 *Works*, VIII, p. 73.

drunkenness brings. When common-sense reason is relaxed, the mind can find room for mystery and awe. "In dreams we are true poets," as Emerson would put it later, in a discussion of the degree to which all men are potential poets so far as their imagination is free and active. Perhaps only in dreams or intoxication then could the poetic potential be actualized in "ecstatic or poetic speech." The prayer we should pray for poets and for all those who desire the vision and gifts of the poet is "O celestial Bacchus! drive them mad."[20] That the god granted the petition for a number of our greatest Emersonian poets, particularly Hart Crane and Roethke, is clear enough—and may well make us pause, as it did Yvor Winters long ago, to ponder the human cost of creative imaginative utterance. Perhaps a prosaic sobriety is to be preferred as less costly. Certainly it is less dangerous to "the seeming-solid walls of use"—of custom, tradition, manners, institutions, authority—which in "Bacchus" are seen as dissolved by the poet's vision. "To be preferred," perhaps; but if Emerson's understanding of the creative processes is essentially correct, at least for a certain kind of poetry, then the choice will not be an easy one to make, will perhaps not even be offered.

It should be possible, it seems to me, to recognize in "Bacchus" a great poetic achievement whatever we may finally think about the wisdom or unwisdom of accepting its vision as a guide to life. Both "Apollonian" and "Dionysian" elements are undeniably real aspects of the rhythmic processes of psychic life. It is only when we are asked to choose between them as dominant life styles that we have, perhaps, if we are fortunate, the option of choosing one or the other. "Bacchus" does not demand that we make this choice, only that we grant the poet his Dionysian vision, though of course it reveals the choice Emerson the man as well as Emerson the poet ideally would have made, a choice not forced on *us* by the poem. Poetry, art, all creative think-

[20] This and the two preceding quotations are from "Poetry and Imagination," pp. 47, 69, 71.

ing are full of ideas dangerous to common sense and a well-ordered life, but many of us are not yet ready to give up the arts and thinking for safety's sake. Of course the danger inherent in the idea expressed in "Bacchus" is real, all the more real because it rests not on some private, distorted fantasy of Emerson's but on deep insights into very important aspects of poetic, and perhaps all, creativity. Granted the poem's subject—the sources and nature of poetic inspiration—I can only suppose that the poem would be less great if its doctrine were less dangerous to the order we quite properly value in our sane and sober moments.

The movement of the poem is controlled from first to last by the paradoxical analogy it maintains between the Christian rite of Holy Communion, which Emerson had long ago refused to go on celebrating, and the Transcendental communion with Reality, which is praised in the poem as greatly to be preferred. At least a half-dozen verbal echoes of the traditional Christian rite are scattered through the poem like sign posts, with the intentions of the service, its symbolic meanings for believers, echoed, criticized by implication, and inverted in the spaces between the signs. By the time Emerson wrote the poem he was far beyond the objections to the service he had explained in his sermon announcing his resignation, but he remembered the rite too well to have any need to look up its words in a Prayer Book. The "elements" of the rite, bread and wine, "symbolizing" for some, "becoming" for others, "the body and blood of Christ," are also the elements of the Transcendental communion described in the poem, though clear water will do in place of wine in one stanza. The chief Scriptural direction for the rite, "This do in remembrance of me," is echoed twice, first in "Winds of remembering," then in "the remembering wine." The Reformation controversy over whether "transubstantiation" or "consubstantiation" better described how the bread and wine were transmuted into the body and blood of Christ to effect "the real presence" is echoed and dismissed in the line that describes the preferred Transcendental elements as "Food which needs no transmuting." The Scriptural "This is my blood, which is shed for you" is also alluded to twice, first in the description of *this* wine as "Blood of the world," then in the characterization of it as "Wine that is shed," by implication not just for "you," that is, believers, but freely for all men, as the rain falls on all. Transcendental communion, in short, was immune to the two chief criticisms that Emerson believed invalidated the Christian rite: it did not rest upon "superstition," upon the credulous acceptance of miracles the Higher Criticism had undermined, and it was not the exclusive property of the faithful.[21]

Yet while wholly avoiding these fatal weaknesses, the new rite accomplishes the same ends. Like the Eucharist or Lord's Supper with its reminders of Christ's suffering and death, Emerson's communion wine is made from grapes that grow "From a nocturnal root" and make the partaker hear the discordancies of "Chaos" as well as the harmonies of music. Bringing with it a realization of death, it brings also the promise of resurrection: "Quickened so, will I unlock / Every crypt of every rock." The rite Emerson describes ends with the same joyful assurance as that brought to believers in the Christian rite: it affirms the victory of life over death, thus working to "cure the old despair" and bring us alive with a vision of "the dancing Pleiads and eternal men."

Thus the poem which began by invoking the kind of awareness that lies at the heart of mystical experience and continued by suggesting what the achievement of such a faith would demand of us, would cost in self-surrender,

21 See "The Lord's Supper," *Works*, XI, pp. 9-29 (*Miscellanies*). Emerson was explicit about his first objection but, speaking to a Christian congregation, tactfully indirect about the second: Christianity's claim on us rests on its superiority as a "moral system," but the rite Emerson was objecting to imputes to Jesus "an authority which he never claimed" [*sic*]. The sermon suggests that Emerson had read his New Testament as selectively as he normally read all books, picking up and remembering only what suited his purposes.

ends in a triumphant paradoxical affirmation of the saving
power of visionary union with the supramundane rhythms
of nature. Knowing that darkness, disorder, and death do
not have the last word, the Transcendental visionary is
ready to participate in the dance of the stars, secure in the
knowledge that his own spirit is above time, above the flowing and melting of the world. Because he has eaten and
drunk of the sources of terror, incorporating them into himself, his faith seems fully earned.[22] The poem is perfectly
and firmly balanced on its central irresolvable paradox, that
only with a full awareness of all the reasons for negation
can a sensitive man make a meaningful affirmation.

Unlike "Bacchus," which all readers have found a char-

[22] Needless to say, in "Bacchus" Emerson does not "argue" for immortality, he simply assumes it as he does in the late essay "Immortality." (The essay is "late" in final composition and publication, but
Emerson put it together, with much help, by searching out passages
he had written on the subject over a period of many years. The faith
in immortality the essay affirms was by no means a late acquisition of
Emerson's.) As he says in the essay, "I mean that I am a better be-
liever, and all serious souls are better believers in immortality, than
we can give grounds for. The real evidence is too subtle, or is higher
than we can write down in propositions, and therefore Wordsworth's
'Ode' is the best modern essay on the subject. We can not prove our
faith by syllogisms."

Emerson did not think of immortality as involving a heaven of
unending duration. "Future state is an illusion for the ever-present
state. It is not length of life but depth of life. It is not duration, but
a taking of the soul out of time. . . ." On this matter, as so often, he
anticipated the thought of the late theologian Paul Tillich.

Faith in immortality, the essay argues, is the only alternative to
nihilism. "The skeptic affirms that the universe is a nest of boxes with
nothing in the last box." The man of faith cannot disprove the skeptical view, but he falls back, not on a "legend"—that is, the story of
Christ's resurrection—but on a firmer "ground of hope," his sense of
"the infinity of the world."

"Bacchus" is, of course, perfectly capable of standing by itself as a
completed and intelligible poem, but a knowledge of the essay can
both extend and clarify our grasp of the cluster of meanings the
poem so compactly and beautifully suggests. See *Works*, VIII, pp.
307-333 (*Letters and Social Aims*).

acteristically Emersonian poem, "Hamatreya" has seemed to some of its readers quite untypical of Emerson in its central *memento mori* theme and its failure to affirm, in any explicit way at least, the possibility of transcending the understanding's world of fact and sense to participate in the visionary realm of spirit. Though its uncharacteristic features are likely to be what we first note about it, it seems to me that further reflection may persuade us that fundamental aspects of Emerson's outlook and sensibility find expression in the poem in a style distinctively Emerson's own, so that the oddities that first impress us come to seem superficial.

Superficial or not, they are of course real in some sense. Unlike such poems as "May-Day," "The Humble-Bee," and "Woodnotes," "Hamatreya" does not illustrate in any obvious way Emerson's conviction that when it fully realizes its potential, poetry "is" faith. Rather than affirming Emerson's faith openly, the poem comes down even more strongly than "Bacchus" does on the necessary humbling, the religious sense of man's utter dependence, that must, Emerson thought, precede any valid affirmation. Meditating on Concord's past and listening to the words of the Earth-Mother as his imagination presents them, leave the speaker in the poem, as he says, no longer "brave." If we stop thinking about the matter at this point, we may well ask, what has happened to the writer who counselled self-reliance and emphasized always the temporal redemption available to man?

It would be oversimplifying somewhat to say that nothing has happened to him except that now he is in touch with, and finding a way to express, a fuller range of his experience and his feelings, but the too-simple reply would I think at least point in the right direction. Anyone who has profited by Whicher's study[23] of Emerson's persistent feeling of powerlessness and his responses to the many tragic

23 Stephen E. Whicher, *Freedom and Fate: An Inner Life of Ralph Waldo Emerson*, Philadelphia, University of Pennsylvania Press, 1953.

losses in his life will be prepared to see in "Hamatreya" an expression of some of the feelings that prompted Emerson often to do what seems to us like whistling in the dark. When his affirmations strike us as most forced, even shrill, they reveal both the strength of his need to affirm and the difficulty of affirming, for anyone with Emerson's outlook and experience. If "Hamatreya" is a stronger poem than "May-Day," as it has seemed to the majority of Emerson's modern readers, it is not because it expresses less of his deeper sensibility but more of it.

The obvious subject of the poem is Concord's history, which, because his own ancestors played a prominent part in it, is also in a sense Emerson's own history. The deeper subject is the meaning of that history. Emerson sometimes thought of himself as "an endless seeker with no past" at his back, but when he meditated on Concord, reading the town records and pondering over the family documents, the self-image as a pastless seeker must have come to seem to him—how consciously, there is no way of knowing—more a symbolic verbal gesture expressive of intention and wish, a sort of programmatic manifesto, than an adequate description of his mixed inner feelings. The *reality* of the past had to be reckoned with, and the attempt to reckon with it aroused the mixed feelings that find expression in the poem. Though the central paradox developed by the poem—that men, even those men who cleared the wilderness, made the land theirs, and settled the town, never did own the earth but the earth owns them—is much more traditional, less peculiarly Emerson's own discovery, than the controlling paradox of "Bacchus," it is still true that in that time and place, only Emerson could have written the poem. This seems to me to be so whether we think of the poem thematically or stylistically, as something said or as something made.

The paradoxes of attachment-detachment that strengthen the poem become clearer, in their genesis at least, if we know something of the historical and biographical facts of

Emerson's relation to Concord and particularly if we read
his "Historical Discourse" on the history of the town, delivered in 1835 just after he moved there, on the occasion of
the celebration of Concord's second centennial.[24] Just the
year before, looking forward to his coming move to the
country town as symbolizing a new beginning in his life
after the traumas of his resignation from the ministry and
Ellen's death, he had written in one of his notebooks, "Hail
to the quiet fields of my fathers!" The address, for which he
made uncharacteristically thorough preparation, conscien-
tiously consulting, as he says in it, every document and
record he could lay hands on, blends factual history,
eulogy, and democratic patriotism with the most tactfully
managed acknowledgment that the town's selection of its
new resident to give the main address of the great occasion
was appropriate. After all, without his ancestors there
might have been no Concord, or it might have had less reason for pride in its past.

Emerson knew this very well and assumes in his address
that his listeners do too. It is not surprising that Peter Bulkeley, the wealthiest and most important of the founding
fathers and Emerson's first Concord ancestor, who is given
first place among the names that make the first line of the
poem, had been singled out for special tribute in the address. The poem's first section condenses those aspects of
the town's real history that had impressed Emerson, offering an interpretation of its facts only as a journalist might,
by emphasis and omission. It lists the actual names of the
settlers[25] and the actual products they raised once they had

[24] "Historical Discourse, at Concord, on the Second Centennial An-
niversary of the Incorporation of the Town, September 12, 1835,"
Works, XI, pp. 33-97 (*Miscellanies*).

[25] Apart from Bulkeley, it is not clear what principle led Emerson
to select just *these* names from the much longer list of founding
fathers given in the address. It seems to me very possible that it was
Emerson's much-maligned poetic "ear" that guided him in selecting
names for the sound of them. There is assonance in B*u*lkeley and
H*u*nt and in W*i*llard and Fl*i*nt; alliteration in *H*unt and *H*osmer;

cleared the land, conveying not only in what it says and does not say about the founders but in the style in which they are described, the *solidity* of their accomplishments, as accomplishments are measured in time, that is, in history. But since, unlike the address, the poem is not a eulogy prepared for delivery before the descendants of those it names, it ends by dissipating, evaporating, the solid "reality" of the past that has been so carefully established, dissipating it by listening to a voice much older than Concord's two centuries of existence. If Emerson had had no reason to feel personal pride in Concord's past and had not known its facts so well, "Hamatreya" would have been a much weaker poem. It might, like "Two Rivers," have barely acknowledged the literal facts of time and space before moving into a transcendent realm of greater significance. In Concord in the thirties, the endless seeker found a past he had no wish wholly to deny and was in no position to ignore.

But if the deeds of Bulkeley and the later ministerial ancestors in Concord occasioned real pride and a sense of identification in Emerson, he could ignore in the address but not in the poem another, contrary, feeling: he was not only a newcomer to the town but intellectually and spiritually an alien to it, past and present, in several senses. As far as present-day Concord was concerned, the Boston-born, Harvard-educated intellectual son of a prominent

---

and a kind of internal "rhyming" for which there is no name in Flin*t* and Hun*t*.

The relevant paragraph in the address reads as follows:

Yet the race survives whilst the individual dies. In the country, without any interference of the law, the agricultural life favors the permanence of families. Here are still around me the lineal descendants of the first settlers of this town. Here is Blood, Flint, Willard, Meriam, Wood, Hosmer, Barrett, Wheeler, Jones, Brown, Buttrick, Brooks, Stow, Hoard, Heywood, Hunt, Miles,—the names of the inhabitants for the first thirty years; and the family is in many cases represented, when the name is not. If the name of Bulkeley is wanting, the honor you have done me this day, in making me your organ, testifies your persevering kindness to his blood (*Works*, XI, p. 34).

Boston minister was moving to a town still composed mostly of farmers, many of them still bearing the original names the poem partially lists and still dominated by the religious beliefs of the fathers. Being asked to give the address was a gratifying recognition of the town's acceptance of him, an acceptance that throughout his life he never ceased to value, but as he pondered the documents, particularly the official town records, with their concentration on births and deaths and the transfers of titles to land, he must have felt an estrangement that was easy enough to ignore in the address but that in the poem, written a few years later, would find expression and exist in conflict with the attachment the poem also expresses, almost, but not quite, cancelling it out in the end.

The founders had very real and visible achievements to their credit, as the address emphasizes fully, and Emerson was no man to despise solid accomplishment; but spiritually, he felt, they had walked in darkness. One of the most interesting parallels between the address and the poem—in the midst of so many differences of attitude and effect—is the way Emerson treats the religion of the founders in the two works. In the address he comes as close as possible to ignoring it, except when he can praise feats of hardihood or signs of firmness of character in his ministerial forebears. In the poem he is licensed to go a step further. If we read the first section of the poem as "history," we find it good literal history in every sense except one: as far as we can tell from the poem, the Puritans had no religion at all, or, if we shift to Tillich's terminology, their "ultimate concern," their "religion," was centered on ownership of land. As an interpretation of Concord's Puritan religious past, the poem is perversely a-historical. And this despite the fact that both Old and New Testaments, as Emerson could not help knowing but apparently found it not to his purposes to remember, repeatedly rebuke the idea of man's "ownership" of God's creation, the earth, holding up in its place the ideal of "stewardship" and accountability, so that even if

the religion of the forefathers was as superstitious and untenable as Emerson thought it to be, it could hardly be
interpreted as exalting pride of ownership. (The "Protestant
ethic" may have encouraged enterprise, but this was not
Emerson's subject either.)

Emerson's mixed feelings, then, toward Concord and its
—and his own ancestors'—past find their way into the poem
in several ways, all of them crucial to the poem's strength
even when modern historical scholarship would find the description the poem offers of the Puritans and their way of
living and thinking even more recognizably a nineteenth-
century interpretation than Hawthorne's in *The Scarlet Letter.* The poem is strengthened by Emerson's sense of the
reality of Concord's past, but the historical interpretation
it offers is "good Emerson" without being "good history."
In the poem, Emerson uses selected facts and very personal
impressions of Concord's history for his own sufficient purposes. That he pictures the founders, for example, as living
oblivious of death when in fact they were at least as pre-
occupied with it as he was is quite irrelevant to the poem's
achievement. What is not irrelevant is that in it he manages
to make the men he names and their lives and achievements
seem utterly real before dissolving their reality by shifting
perspective. First, actual men, actual, weighty products of
their efforts; then, death's negation; then, the sibylline assurances of the "Earth-Song" telling us that though men dis-
appear, "Earth endures" and "Stars abide," so that history
contains reasons for hope even while it rebukes man's delusion of permanence. The bravery the speaker has lost by the
end of the poem turns out to have been more like bravado
than like true courage. Its loss is necessary if there is to be
a faith not based on delusion, as, in Emerson's view, that of
the founding fathers was, but on Truth as the earth speaks
it. The founders were strong, admirable, hardy men; Concord town is their visible monument; but their land-hunger
was a kind of avarice, and their practicality a kind of blind-
ness. They found in nature nothing to awaken religious

awe, only a wilderness to be subdued. At the end of the
poem the speaker is far beyond them in understanding:

> When I heard the Earth-song,
> I was no longer brave;
> My avarice cooled
> Like lust in the chill of the grave.

The feeling behind these lines is religious awe, or fear, but
not despair. The speaker has lost the assurances that made
the founders "brave," but, in the poem's terms, he is more
truly religious than they. Emerson could not have said this
in the address, but the poem says it.

The free use, and breaking, of traditional verse forms is
as effective in "Hamatreya" as in any poem Emerson ever
wrote. Though blank verse predominates in the opening
section, the first and third lines subordinate the traditional
form to the facts, implying that there is poetry enough in
these bare lists of names and farm products. Neither line
can be scanned by any traditional prosodic system, and the
poem is stronger for that fact. The blank verse is also
broken by two later lines, each of which deserves the special emphasis the breaking gives it: "Clear of the grave" and
"Hear what the Earth says." This is functional form as
Emerson understood it, "metre-making argument."

In the second section, the Earth speaks in dipodic lines
with irregular rhyme—in short, in no traditional poetic art
form at all—announcing the verities in the simplest, most
direct way possible. If "fact" had appeared to dictate the
form of the poem's first and third lines, here it is artless,
riddling "wisdom" that seems in control:

> 'Mine and yours;
> Mine, not yours.
> Earth endures;
> Stars abide — .'

It seems appropriate, too, that in the end, after the Earth
finishes her song, the speaker should drop the original art
form—blank verse—of his earlier reflections and speak in

a way that implies that he has not only absorbed the Earth's wisdom but has been affected by her tone. The last four lines of the poem suggest both the dipodic tradition Emerson associated with the "primitive" and "bardic" and a free version of the Common Meter, which had roughly the same associations for him.[26] Dipodics are suggested by the fact that there are only two strong stresses in each of the first three lines, Common Meter by the a-b-c-b rhyme scheme and by the longer, three-stress, last line. The final stanza is thus Emerson's "invention," dictated by the whole "argument" of the poem.

All this is "good Emerson," but one feature of the poem is unusual enough to deserve brief comment. In "Hamatreya" paradox is supplemented by, or moves into, rhetorical irony in a very effective way. The "landlords" of the opening lines prove not to be "lords" of the "land" after all, though they think they are.[27] They and their land become mingled in their imaginations, we are told, until they can imagine that it knows them as they know it, knows them as a dog knows its master. There is something in common, the

[26] See, for example, the "Bards and Trouveurs" section of "Poetry and Imagination" and Strauch's "The Mind's Voice. . . ." Strauch discusses the "Bardic" and "runic" sources of Emerson's mature poetic theory and practice separately, but it seems to me that the two tended to coalesce in Emerson's mind. Both were outside the conventions of traditional art-poetry, both were "primitive" and "natural," and both were associated with mysterious or riddling wisdom of a sort inaccessible to common-sense views or to ordinary reasonableness.

[27] With his usual tact and shrewdness, Emerson tempered his address to the occasion, which did not call for irony or for criticism of Concord's early history. What he says about the landlords in the poem had come out this way in the address: "And the people truly feel that they are lords of the soil." Again, though he avoids characterizing the religious faith of the forefathers, he manages, as he moves into his conclusion, to praise their piety: "I have had much opportunity of access to anecdotes of families, and I believe this town to have been the dwelling place, in all times since its planting, of pious and excellent persons . . ." (*Works*, XI, pp. 52, 88).

landlords are said to fancy, between owner and owned: " 'we sympathize; / And, I affirm, my actions smack of the soil.' " What the settlers "know" turns out to be illusory, and what they solemnly "affirm" turns out to be true, but in a sense quite opposite from what they intend: when death has added the owner to his land, his decaying body becomes "a lump of mould the more." Only then does his "fancy" that he and the land have something in common, that they "sympathize," acquire any real truth. A lump of flesh in the grave may be said literally to "smack of the soil," as decay goes on, until finally it is inseparable from the soil, the two becoming one, though in a different sense from that imagined by the founders.

The paradoxes "Brahma" rests on and develops are more obviously characteristic of Emerson than those of "Hamatreya," though I think it has not been often enough noted that in its versification the poem is more typical of minor than of major Emerson. Be that as it may, both Victorian and later readers have generally found this one of Emerson's strongest poems, whether they liked or detested its "doctrines." Until recently, at least, it has generally aroused very strong responses, either positive or negative. A favorite of some, it has seemed either ridiculous or dangerous to others. The one thing this wholly paradoxical poem seems never to have struck any of its readers as being is innocuous. If we read it literally rather than as paradox, it appears to express views very close to some of the most unattractive aspects of ancient Gnosticism.[28] The most unsympathetic reader may be prompted to ask about it what Santayana asked about the shock effect of Emerson's work as a whole, "Was not the startling effect of much of his writing due to its contradiction to tradition and to common sense?"[29] But even such a reaction, in effect denying "truth-speaking"

[28] See Hans Jonas, *The Gnostic Religion*, Second Edition, Revised, Boston, Beacon Press, 1963, chap. II, esp. pp. 37-47.
[29] George Santayana, "Emerson," in *Interpretations of Poetry and Religion*.

value to the poem, would be evidence that the reader had been forced to take it seriously enough to try to explain its effect on him. Every aspect of the poem, from its tone to its cadences, demands that it be taken seriously, as revelation, either genuine or spurious. In Emerson's day the religiously orthodox quite correctly, from their point of view, found its paradoxes blasphemously contradictory of the central articles of their faith, while Transcendental readers tended to value it for its strong rebuke to what seemed to them an untenable and dying religious anthropomorphism. In our day, readers who are neither orthodox Christians nor Transcendentalists may recognize the poem as an exercise in paradoxy without responding to it strongly either way, positively or negatively. To an extent that may weaken the poem for many of us, the paradoxes depend for their effectiveness on three assumptions in the minds of readers that are far less common now than in Emerson's day: that the distinctions the god's voice mocks at are perfectly clear to us in "real life"; that God exists, not as part of a lost worldview but as a present reality; and that he who finds God will go to Heaven. To the contemporary reader who holds none of these beliefs, the poem's paradoxes may seem neither shocking nor revealing.

"Brahma" is brief enough to quote entire:

> If the red slayer think he slays,
>   Or if the slain think he is slain,
> They know not well the subtle ways
>   I keep, and pass, and turn again.
>
> Far or forgot to me is near;
>   Shadow and sunlight are the same;
> The vanished gods to me appear;
>   And one to me are shame and fame.
>
> They reckon ill who leave me out;
>   When me they fly, I am the wings;
> I am the doubter and the doubt,
>   And I the hymn the Brahmin sings.

The strong gods pine for my abode,
And pine in vain the sacred Seven;
But thou, meek lover of the good!
Find me, and turn thy back on heaven.

Some of the praise the poem has received over the years, particularly by academic critics, seems to me based on the wrong reasons—for example, the dramatic unity created by the fact that the poem consists of the words of a single speaker explaining his ways to man; the regularity of the prosodic structure and the end rhyming, with only one slant rhyme, "abode–good"; and the reinforcement of sense afforded by the "verbal music" of the internal chiming and rhyming, as in the alliteration of "Far or forgot"; the consonantal rhyming, as in "pine in vain"; and the assonantal play on similar vowel sounds that is too constant a feature of the verse to require illustrative quotation.

The "wrong" reasons? I do not mean to suggest that there is anything illegitimate in a poet's use of such traditional features of heightened poetic language, only that the style here is uncharacteristic of Emerson in his greatest poems and that therefore to praise the poem for it is to imply that when he writes as he usually does when he writes at his best, as in "Merlin," "Bacchus," and "Hamatreya," he must be writing poorly. In its formal characteristics "Brahma" is a very regular and traditional poem, perfectly free of the many "faults" Emerson's early critics delighted to point out in his verse, but its style is only one of several Emerson could use, and not the one we find in most of his greatest poems.

Emerson contributed "Brahma" to the first issue of *The Atlantic Monthly* in November, 1857, when he was deeply involved in the issues that would soon lead to the Civil War. To him the Northern cause had come, later than to others like Whittier and Garrison, to seem a moral crusade. Soon Christian churches in the two regions would be sending up a clamor of petitions to God for victory in their righteous causes, very much in the manner described later in Stephen

Crane's poem on the subject. Emerson had become fully
convinced that a victory of the Union cause was essential
to the triumph of right over wrong, but at the same time he
was still as much convinced as ever of the truth of what he
had said many years earlier in "The Bohemian Hymn," that
"the Universal Friend / Doth as far transcend / An angel
as a worm," so that "The measure of the eternal Mind" cannot be found in hymn or prayer or church. If "The great
Idea baffles wit" and "Language falters under it," then invoking divine sanction for even the most worthy of our
causes smacks of blasphemy. Only the transhuman or su-
prahuman Real deserves our full allegiance. I suspect that
the voice in the poem rebuking man, reminding him of the
god's utter transcendence, gets its sharpness of tone from
Emerson's awareness of the conflict within himself between
the impulse toward commitment and the impulse to with-
draw into contemplation of the Real. Emerson was usually
gentle in his rebukes to others, sharp with himself.

Though "Brahma" is a purer expression of Emerson's
growing enthusiasm for Oriental wisdom than "Hamatreya," even this poem does not suggest a total break with
all aspects of his religious heritage, as comments on it have
usually tended to suggest. In his notebook the poem is entitled "The Song of the Soul," a title that has the advantage
of reminding us that Emerson's soul had been singing similar melodies in a more subdued tone for a long time. There
were elements stressing the absoluteness of God's transcendence in the Neoplatonic writings that had meant so
much to him in the years when he was finding himself, and
the mysticism he valued had often led in the past to
an emphasis on God's otherness, his complete reversal of all
the world's values. Puritanism itself had rebuked the hu-
manizing tendencies of the Catholic church by emphasizing
God's absolute power and the inability of unaided reason
to reach him or merely human virtue to impress him.

But it could be argued that the thrust of the poem is not
so much in these directions as it is toward Quietism, which

also has a long history as a submerged minor strain in Western piety. Christian forms of mysticism have often, though of course not always, encouraged passive contemplation, set a higher value on wordless prayers of praise and thanksgiving than on specific petitions, and seen annihilation of the human will as the necessary condition for the beatific vision. To find such a point of view expressed by one who felt no need to turn to Oriental scripture for support for it, we need look no further than Emerson's friend and one-time protégé Jones Very, the Christ-centered Unitarian mystic. The most important difference, thematically, between some of Very's poems and "Brahma" is that while Very plays down the moral antinomianism that would seem to be implicit in his faith, Emerson in "Brahma" finds shocking ways to emphasize it.

Still, it is possible to exaggerate the poem's paradoxical annihilation of moral and all other distinctions, its equation of slayer and slain, light and dark, far and near, doubt and faith. The paradoxes of the first three stanzas are shocking denials of common decency and common sense, but they are such clear denials of the "obvious" that they seem to demand a "higher truth" to support them. That higher truth is paradoxically suggested in the last stanza's theological paradox, which, if it works, "justifies" the earlier ethical, spatial-temporal, and logical paradoxes by subsuming them. "Find me, and turn thy back on heaven."

If finding the god makes us willing to turn our backs on heaven, then it is not only our physical, logical, and moral distinctions but our religious ideas also, and chiefly, that need first to be negated and then redefined. The heaven of our dreams, which even the "strong gods" pine for in vain, can be and often popularly has been a dream of the continuation forever of the more satisfactory aspects of our temporally and spatially bounded experience, a "utopia" (nowhere) in which the perpetuation of the self is guaranteed. If this is what "heaven" means to us, as Emerson seems in the poem to assume, it could be viewed as more a betrayal than an expression of our religious heritage. If annihilation of the will is a condition of the beatific vision, one who has really found the Most High will be beyond pining for such a heaven. "Brahma" is Emerson's strongest expression of his religious intuitions, intuitions he found inexpressible except in the form of paradoxes deriving ultimately from the Medieval and Renaissance tradition of "negative theology."[30]

[30] Though, as I have suggested, it seems to me clear that Emerson came to understand and value paradoxy through his reading in Western writers, theologians, and mystics, a number of whom became his favorite authors, still it is interesting to note that in his later reading in Oriental scriptures he would have found confirmation of his already-established belief that paradox was a valid way of thinking and writing, as he undoubtedly found confirmation of other articles of his faith. See, for example, Aldous Huxley's summation of the "second doctrine" of the "Perennial Philosophy" in his Introduction to *The Song of God: Bhagavad-Gita*, Mentor Classics, p. 15. See also Alistair Kee, *The Way of Transcendence*, Penguin Books, 1971, p. 15, and W. T. Stace, *Mysticism and Philosophy*, New York, Macmillan, 1961, *passim*.

CHAPTER IV

The Poetry of the Prose

After we have granted Emerson his rare but impressive triumphs in verse, and granted too that a sympathetic reading of his collected poems today would be likely to discover a larger number of successful poems, or parts of poems, than critics in the past have generally allowed him, we may still find ourselves agreeing with perhaps his most perceptive early critic, Chapman, that he is more often at his poetic best in his prose than in his verse. The reasons given by the detractors of his verse may strike us as unsatisfactory today, for we are not likely to demand either Tennysonian melodiousness or Eliotic irony in the verse that pleases us, but I at least cannot entirely dispel my sense that the bulk of the verse confirms Henry James's impression that in Emerson we have a writer who has not found but seems to be seeking his form. Often, I should say, Emerson's prose is not only more imaginative, richer in its suggestive power and so in the kinds of meaning poetry has, but even more "musical," more pleasing in its cadences, than his verse.

It would be easier to explain why this is so if we could agree with Arnold and Lowell and their critical followers that the "rules" of good verse are fixed and known, or with certain contemporary critics that only "organic form"—the "metre-making argument" of Emerson's theory—is possible for the modern poet. But if both these conceptions of "legitimacy" must be rejected, no easy single answer presents itself to the question of why Emerson's verse has seemed strikingly uneven in quality to so many sympathetic readers in different periods, readers who approached it with quite different models of "good poetry" in mind. We are left with our impression that Emerson is often stylistically uneasy and imaginatively not at his best in much of his verse.

The conviction that all previous efforts to explain this impression have failed to explain, or have explained too much, prevents me from offering yet another single explanation. Where Arnold and Lowell, Matthiessen and Whicher have failed, I have no hope of succeeding. Still, not to back away from the problem as simply too difficult, I shall offer, very tentatively, several judgments that repeated rereadings of the whole body of verse have seemed to confirm.

One trouble with much of the verse, it seems to me, is that what in the great poems seems a necessary and functional breaking of the form seems in the weaker poems and passages to be arbitrary, fitful, unrelated to what the poem is saying. When a form seems to be preventing a writer from saying what he wants to say and so must be abandoned intermittently, form and content have come apart. At its poorest, Emerson's verse forces us alternately to try to enjoy jingles and to admire hoarse gnomic utterances. We can only conclude that, whether consciously or not, Emerson was often uneasy within the traditional rhyming verse forms he used, finding it impossible to say what he wanted to say within them. In the poems of his maturity, blank verse seems to me the only traditional form he always handles with ease and perfect control, with perfected "craftsmanship," in short.

The purely formal weakness of a good deal of his verse that bothers me the most is not of course the frequency of slant or "imperfect" rhymes but the forced quality of much of his rhyming, even when the rhymes themselves are "perfect." At times it seems that there is nothing, neither sense nor syntax, that Emerson is not willing to sacrifice to achieve a rhyme. Of course when he did this it was not any excessive respect for an arbitrary poetic convention that seemed to him to justify it. He believed and said repeatedly that rhyming in verse was one of the chief ways in which the form of poetry reflected the only "permanencies" of Nature's perpetual flowing. The poet's rhymes were echoes of nature's periodic returns and polarities. Over and over again from youth to age Emerson recorded in both verse and prose his conviction that in rhyming his poems the poet is following the example set by Nature. Being able to hear Nature's rhymes where others heard only disordered sounds seemed to him, as he put it in "Beauty," to be indeed one of the chief tests of the true poet:

> He heard a voice none else could hear
> From centred and from errant sphere.
> The quaking earth did quake in rhyme,
> Seas ebbed and flowed in epic chime.

If nature herself "rounds with rhyme her every rune," then it is not an impulse to artifice but true inspiration that re-sults in the poet's "lofty rhymes, / Of things with things, of times with times." The poet will inevitably, in his inspired moments, find his thoughts coming to him "In equal couples mated, / Or else alternated"—in either couplets or quat-rains, in short.

Though this idea of Emerson's helps to explain why he felt justified in going to the lengths he did to achieve some of his rhymes, it is unlikely to make them seem any less dis-tressing to the modern reader, partly perhaps because we may feel that at this point Emerson is making too easy an equation of the natural and the aesthetic, partly because it may seem to us that despite the obvious polarities of day and night, light and dark, up and down, birth and death, and all the rest, it is not clear that there are not breaks, dis-continuities, and disorders in nature that cannot be sub-sumed under any orderly laws of predictable echo and re-turn. Even if we were to accept Emerson's faith that Nature always "rhymes," we might object that a poem's rhymes should seem as natural and unforced as Nature's. If the poet is obliged to invert the normal word order of spoken lan-guage, to tinker with syntax until the meaning becomes diffi-cult to determine, or even to wrench the agreed-upon mean-ings of words for no other apparent reason than to make a

rhyme, he must not, from Emerson's own point of view, have
listened carefully enough or long enough to Nature.

A single glaring example of the awkwardness or worse of
some of Emerson's rhyming in his weaker poems should be
sufficient. "My Garden" records his pleasure in the woodlot
on the shores of Walden pond he purchased and enjoyed
visiting, where Thoreau would later be permitted to build
his cabin. The land was Emerson's, yet in a sense not his but
Nature's, since natural processes of growth and decay went
on here without any interference from man in his role as
either sower or reaper:

> The sowers made haste to depart,—
> The wind and the birds which sowed it;
> Not for fame, nor by rules of art,
> Planted these, and tempests flowed it.

Here the "depart–art" rhyme is achieved at the cost of an
inversion of word order that seems awkward and makes for
difficult reading, while the ludicrous "sowed it–flowed it"
rhyme is obtained only by sacrificing good diction and good
sense. By "flowed it" Emerson presumably means "watered"
the "garden" in which the wind and the birds had accom-
plished the "planting" of the seeds. But "flow" is an intransitive verb: "the river flows." When it is used transitively, as
it rarely is, it means "to cause to flow." Neither sense will fit
here. A poet may coin words, of course, but only if he seems
to know what he is about, to be firmly in control of his
medium.

In another sense too the traditional verse forms Emerson
most often used seem in his weaker verse to be hindering
rather than helping the expression of his thought, particularly in some of the poems in which he used his favorite
tetrameter couplets with the greatest regularity. It is no
mere coincidence that neoclassic writers in the "Age of Reason" preferred above all other forms pentameter or tetrameter couplets. Both are closed forms, tight, tidy, logical
forms the mere "understanding" can produce and appreci-

ate most naturally. But Emerson's poems are seldom content to try to convey what can be grasped by the mere understanding. Their substance is usually the higher illuminations apprehensible only to imaginative "Reason," as he called it in the early years, following Coleridge's distinction. The Reason perceives a reality that eludes the understanding, a wild, flowing, "fugacious" world in which stability, solidity, and permanence (except the permanence of Nature's cyclical returns and of the Spiritual Laws) are all equally illusions, a world in which "thin or solid, everything is in flight," a world in which the poet realizes that even "his own body is a fleeing apparition,—his personality as fugitive as the trope he employs." Imagination sees that "The nature of things is flowing, a metamorphosis," but can this Heraclitean vision be adequately conveyed or evoked in couplets, in which the implication of the closed form is that the world is limited, regular, and predictable, perfectly capable of being grasped by the understanding? Perhaps, but Emerson's weaker poems at least suggest that these forms he had learned to manage in youth and continued to use in age were not wholly suited to express the Heraclitean vision of his maturity, or at least that aspect of it beyond the predictable polarities.

A very different weakness I seem to find in Emerson's verse when he is not writing at his best is the "free-floating" quality of the imagination in it. Emerson felt that poetry set him free to be as fanciful as his mood prompted. "You shall not speak ideal truth in prose uncontradicted: you may in verse," he believed, as he put it in "Poetry and Imagination." But the reader who takes poetry seriously, as Emerson did, is not likely to feel that the poet gains total immunity from the danger of having his opinions contradicted simply by expressing them in verse form, however great the distance may be between the values of propositional logic and those of poetry. Whatever immunity to contradiction the poet may have, his poem must seem to earn for him. In his highest flights toward the Ideal, the poet must not seem

to lose touch with fact, as Emerson knew and often said. His
dictum in the same late great essay that "The restraining
grace of common-sense is the mark of all the valid minds,"
not excluding presumably the mind of the poet, would seem
to offer an even more specific control over unchecked imaginative flights.

But the fact is, it seems to me, that there is too little "common-sense," too little that the understanding can grasp before yielding to the higher authority of Reason or the Imagination, in many of Emerson's poems, including, I should
say, in two of his longest and most ambitious, "Wood-notes"
and "May-Day." Theoretically Emerson knew that the poet
like the rest of us must live in two worlds at once, not confusing or mixing them, not losing touch with the actual even
though it is the chief use of poetry at its best to take us into
the world of the Ideal. He is emphatic about this in "Poetry
and Imagination" and implies it in "The Poet" and elsewhere. But practically, Emerson needed the restraint offered by the possibility of contradiction. Particularly when
he contemplated Nature, his imagination found no difficulty
at all in soaring. What it needed was not unleashing, a
greater freedom, but a firmer tie to the earth, to "the seeming-solid walls" of matter and sense where the understanding finds its home.

On the lecture platform where the essays were tried out,
the visible presence of an audience that must be at least impressed if not persuaded provided the needed checkrein.
That is one of the reasons as I see it why much of the best
of Emerson's poetry is to be found not in his verse but in his
prose. He never wavered in his belief that poetry is the
highest art, and he thought that "The critic, the philosopher, is a failed poet." "God himself does not speak in
prose,"[1] just because the truest revelations proceed from
imagination's realm. But for a poet whose imagination

---

[1] The quotations in this and the three preceding paragraphs are all
from "Poetry and Imagination," *Letters and Social Aims, Works,* VIII.

needed discipline to keep it from becoming flights of fancy, a poet whose tendency to soar into wish-dream was very strong, "the fear of contradiction" could provide a discipline less irksome to him than that provided by the verse forms that both long practice and a part of his theory recommended to him. There is no need to suppose that he thought this whole matter out and made a conscious choice to give most of his effort to prose, even though as the years went by he became increasingly aware of the gap between his poetic ideals and his own achievement of them in verse. Prose was a choice forced on him both by the need to make a living on the lecture platform and by his diminishing hope of achieving power and recognition for greatness as a poet. But if the choice was "destined" rather than free, destiny, as he so often said, may prove, when accepted, to be a blessing in disguise.

Emerson's ideas about the relations between poetry (that is, verse) and prose seem to have undergone no essential change in the years between "The Poet" and the publication of "Poetry and Imagination," which was put together and partly written late, though portions of it had been written much earlier. Early and late, Emerson thought of poetry as the art form with the greatest expressive possibilities and certainly a "higher" form than even the most artful prose. Poetry seemed to him more capable than prose of expressing the Ideal, the ultimately Real that prosaic eyes could not see but the vision of the poet could make available to us. The same distinction between poetry and prose in the power to lift us to the Ideal could be used to distinguish greater from lesser poets. In the early *Dial* essay "Thoughts on Modern Literature" Emerson finds Goethe perhaps the greatest modern writer, praising him in unqualified terms for his intelligence, his vast learning, and his realism but finding him falling short of the highest achievement because his works imply that he did not know that "the ideal is truer

than the actual." Great as he is, Goethe seems to Emerson
always to fall short of "the miracles of poetry" just because
he was never visited by "the transcendent muse." His poetry
therefore never becomes "artful thunder"; it remains no
more, finally, than "the gilding of the chain" of "fate." "Let
him pass."[2] The same criterion is at work, though less explicitly and in less specifically Transcendental terms, in the
discussion of bardic poetry in the very late "Poetry and
Imagination" and elsewhere in the essay.

Early and late too, noetic or visionary imagination is the
poet's distinguishing gift, and its presence or absence can
be used to distinguish greater from lesser poetry as well as
poetry from prose. Imagination is at once, and ambiguous-
ly, "a high kind of seeing" and a power of invention or creation. The imagination is at home with "tropes" in a world
in which reality itself is a vast trope, so that just because it
is not bound by the "literal," poetry has ultimately more
"veracity" of the kind that matters most to us than has
prose. Seeing connections, analogies, "correspondences"
where prosaic vision sees only multiplicity, differences, and
disorder, the poetic imagination "reattaches things to nature and the Whole," the many to the One, and thus finds
meaning in the apparent meaninglessness of ordinary experience. The imagination transfigures the "actual" by seeing in it the "possible." This is why only the poet can save
us.

Verse is the form in which the poetic imagination normally finds its best expression, Emerson thought, but prose
could move toward becoming poetry insofar as imagination
was in control. Emerson implies this in "Poetry and Imag-

2 "Thoughts on Modern Literature," *Natural History of Intellect,
Works,* XII, pp. 196-198. On the two later occasions when he discussed
Goethe, Emerson gave no evidence of having essentially changed his
mind. In the chapter on Goethe in *Representative Men* he softens the
expression of his criticisms somewhat without retracting them, while
the remarks on *Faust* in the late "Poetry and Imagination" are if anything more severe than the 1840 strictures.

ination" when he lists Swedenborg among his favorite poets, along with Milton, Herbert, Wordsworth and others. A little later he makes the implication explicit:

> There are also prose poets. Thomas Taylor, the Platonist, for instance, is really a better man of imagination, a better poet, or perhaps I should say a better feeder to a poet, than any man between Milton and Wordsworth. Thomas Moore had the magnanimity to say, "If Burke and Bacon were not poets (measured lines not being necessary to constitute one), he did not know what poetry meant."[3]

The chief sign that the imagination is at work, whether in verse or in prose, to produce poetry, Emerson thought, is the presence of figurative language. In the lecture-essay "Eloquence," for example, Emerson first confesses that the power of an orator over his audience must remain as much a mystery as the power of a poem over its reader, then goes on to offer two bits of practical advice: be sure of your facts, which must be new to the listeners, and use imagery in presenting and interpreting them:

> Imagery. The orator must be, to a certain extent, a poet. We are such imaginative creatures that nothing so works on the human mind, barbarous or civil, as a trope. Condense some daily experience into a glowing symbol, and an audience is electrified. . . . Put the argument into a concrete shape, into an image,—some hard phrase, round and solid as a ball, which they can see and handle and carry home with them,—and the cause is half won.[4]

But imagery was not the only poetic resource available to the writer of prose. In "Poetry and Imagination" Emerson speaks of what he calls "iterations of phrase," meaning repeated parallel constructions, as "another form of rhyme," then illustrates with a passage of rhythmic prose. Perhaps as a student of Blair's *Rhetoric* speaking to those who had

[3] *Works*, VIII, p. 52.
[4] "Eloquence," *Society and Solitude, Works*, VII, p. 89. Another lecture with the same title may be found in *Letters and Social Aims*.

also been brought up on classical rhetoric, Emerson did not think it necessary to mention the other tropes that heightened prose and verse had in common, but his own poetic prose illustrates most of them. When he wrote on subjects that most closely concerned him and stimulated his imagination, he often seems to be straining at the limits of prose.

"The basis of poetry is language, which is material only on one side," Emerson says in "Art," succinctly reformulating an idea he had first expressed in *Nature* (1836) and later expanded upon in "The Poet." He continues, "It is a demigod. But being applied primarily to the common necessities of man, it is not new-created by the poet for his own ends."[5] The passage reminds us of the warning in "The Poet" against the reification of symbols Emerson had found the mystics guilty of. (The mystic "nails a symbol to one sense . . . all symbols are fluxional; all language is vehicular and transitive, and is good, as ferries and horses are, for conveyance, not as farms and houses are, for homestead.") The poet avails himself of the plasticity of language, refreshing it thus and renewing its power to convey, without supposing that he is creating *ex nihilo* what is dis-covered and thus conveyed. The imagination of the poet, at home with "tropes" as it is, turns out, not surprisingly, to be the best reader of Nature's forms, for "Nature itself is a vast trope," and "All thinking is analogizing."[6]

This is a Transcendental theory of linguistic symbolism, to be sure, and it seems doubtful that there are very many full-fledged Transcendentalists among Emerson's readers today. Fortunately it is not necessary that we be full-fledged metaphysical Transcendentalists in order to see how Emerson's theory works for him not just in the best of his verse but in the best of his prose too. The theory throws great emphasis on the suggestive, the evocative power of in-

5 *Works*, VII, p. 47.
6 "Poetry and Imagination," *Works*, VIII, p. 20.

dividual words and images and minimizes the importance of the larger structures that contain them, implying that the architectonics of poetry or poetic prose are hardly more than a sop to the mere understanding. One effect of this concept of linguistic symbolism may be seen in the often remarked fragmentary effect of much of both the poetry and the prose, but another is the brilliantly evocative and wholly poetic effect of the best of the prose, where it is possible just because the theory of symbolism which controls it has as little to do with logical argument as it has to do with the conventions of verse form. A comparison of some passages on the same subjects in verse and prose may make this clearer.

Many years ago now Bliss Perry in *Emerson Today* (1931), in the course of a sympathetic, sensitive, and judicious evaluation of Emerson's achievement in verse, made the point that "there will always be some readers who discover the real Emerson in his poetry, as there will always be others who prefer to find their Emerson in his *Journals* or *Essays*." He illustrates the point first by comparing a passage in the Channing Ode with a quoted Journal passage that seemed to Perry to make the verse passage clearer, then by asserting, without benefit of quotation, that "The prose draft of his rhymed poem 'Two Rivers,' for instance, seems to many readers to possess a more delicate harmony than the metrical version."[7] The *clarity* of Emerson's thought as such is not the question I am trying to pursue, so the first illustration may be ignored, but the second one seems very much to the point—and I find myself agreeing with Perry's judgment in the matter.

Writing nearly a half century before Perry, in the chapter on Emerson's poems in his book-length tribute to his friend, Oliver Wendell Holmes also compared prose and verse, treating the same subject to reach the opposite conclusion from Perry's. After quoting a single sentence from

[7] Bliss Perry, *Emerson Today*, pp. 84-85.

the essay "Works and Days" ("The days are ever divine as
to the first Aryans"), he quotes the whole poem "Days" and
finds it richer and more meaningful than the prose sentence,
thus justifying his earlier assertion that Emerson's prose is
often highly poetical, but his verse is "something more than
the most imaginative and rhetorical passages of his prose."[8]
Since Holmes does not specify what the "something more"
is, it is hard to disagree with this, but we might note that
comparing a whole poem with a single short sentence of
prose is not likely to prove anything, particularly when the
sentence is excerpted from a twenty-five page essay in
which the first eight and a half pages treat "works" while all
the rest treat the nature and quality of "days." It seems to
me that if Holmes had quoted more extensively from the
essay—one of Emerson's best, and too little known—he
might well have reached the opposite conclusion. At any
rate, I should like to try his experiment again, only this time
giving the essay a fairer chance to speak to us.

"Days" is of course very well known, but it might be well
to have it all freshly in mind. Here it is, complete:

> Daughters of Time, the hypocritic Days,
> Muffled and dumb like barefoot dervishes,
> And marching single in an endless file,
> Bring diadems and fagots in their hands.
> To each they offer gifts after his will,
> Bread, kingdoms, stars, and sky that holds them all.
> I, in my pleached garden, watched the pomp,
> Forgot my morning wishes, hastily
> Took a few herbs and apples, and the Day
> Turned and departed silent. I, too late,
> Under her solemn fillet saw the scorn.

[8] O. W. Holmes, *Ralph Waldo Emerson*, p. 311. Interestingly
enough, John Jay Chapman about a dozen years later in his brilliant
response to and assessment of Emerson also compared "Days" with
its "prose version" in "Works and Days" and came to the same conclusion that Holmes had come to, that the prose is "inferior." But
for Chapman this was an exception to the general rule that Emerson's
poems "are overshadowed by the greatness of his prose." (*Emerson
and Other Essays*, pp. 94-95, 84.)

Contemporary readers brought up on Symbolist poetry find themselves tempted to overread or misread this poem, especially if they take the gifts as symbols in the modern sense, with all the attached literary and mythological meanings they have gathered through the ages. But external evidence makes Emerson's intention clear enough. He was an enthusiastic orchardist who prided himself on his fruit trees, and herbs to him still connoted plants with real or supposed medicinal properties. Thus his choice of herbs and apples was unworthy, merely practical, thoroughly untranscendental. From his own point of view he deserved the scorn he saw, for despite his morning wishes he had chosen downward, not skyward. Too often, he confided frequently in his Journal, his days were so filled with routine trivialities that there was no time to cultivate the epiphanies he desired, the revelations he associated particularly with woods and stars and sky. If "herbs and apples" seem to us at least as attractive choices as stars and sky, to say nothing of their being more attainable, so that the poem begins to seem ambiguous, there are many reasons for doubting that Emerson intended any such ambiguity. The more ambiguous the poem seems to us, the more we must be tempted to judge that Emerson failed to embody in the poem the associations with the ideal that stars and sky carried for him here as they had earlier in the opening paragraph of *Nature*. The poem is intended to mean that our days are often uninspired but might well be filled with meaning if we dared to follow our morning wishes. The emotion left with us by the poem should be regret at having lowered our sights, having failed to live more meaningfully.

Since the relevant part of the essay is far too long to quote entire, I shall try to convey some of the poetry of it by mingled excerpt and paraphrase.[9] In the opening third of the piece Emerson first describes and praises the "works" that his own time was distinguished for, particularly the

[9] "Works and Days," *Society and Solitude, Works*, VII, pp. 151-177, *passim*.

scientific and technological advances of the nineteenth century, the mills and railways and telegraphs. "Civilization
mounts and climbs," it seems. But then he wonders how significant all this material progress is. Perhaps "the machine
unmakes the man," the machinist becoming a machine.
What have all these impressive advances done for "character," what have they contributed to enriching our lives or
making us better individual people? Reminding us of
Hawthorne, as well as Thoreau, Emerson doubts that the
steam engine will save us. Of what use then the much-
vaunted Progress?

> 'Tis too plain that with the material power the moral prog-
> ress has not kept pace. It appears that we have not made a
> judicious investment. Works and days were offered us,
> and we took works . . . we must look deeper for our salva-
> tion than to steam, photographs, balloons or astronomy.

The second and much longer part of the essay begins
with praise of Hesiod's poem "Works and Days," which
Emerson finds "full of piety as well as prudence" but somewhat lacking in depth: the poet "has not pushed his study
of days into such inquiry and analysis as they invite." Emerson then offers his own "analysis" of what days are and what
kind of "wealth" they offer us, though we shall be disap-
pointed if we expect the "analysis" to follow the pattern of
logical discourse. Instead, the style from this point on becomes noticeably more rhythmic and metaphoric at once.
We are treated to a veritable shower of metaphors and
other tropes that together constitute a phenomenological
description of a day in our lives as it is and as it might be.
The discussion begins prosaically enough:

> A farmer said "he should like to have all the land that
> joined his own." Bonaparte, who had the same appetite,
> endeavored to make the Mediterranean a French lake. . . .

But the farmer and Bonaparte, identifying wealth with
ownership of land, have too little imagination to understand

the riches offered us by the moments of time we call our days:

> . . . He only is rich who owns the day. There is no king, rich man, fairy, or demon who possesses such power as that. The days are ever divine as to the first Aryans. They are of the least pretension and of the greatest capacity of anything that exists. They come and go like muffled and veiled figures, sent from a distant friendly party; but they say nothing, and if we do not use the gifts they bring, they carry them as silently away.

Here we have the central image of the poem, the days as veiled silent figures offering gifts, but what does Emerson mean by calling them "divine"? Later sentences in the long meditation clarify what he means. "The days are made on a loom whereof the warp and woof are past and future time." The gifts they offer are "the treasures Nature spent itself to amass" through unimaginable aeons of time,

> . . . which all strata go to form, which the prior races, from infusory and saurian, existed to ripen; the surrounding plastic natures; the earth with its foods; the intellectual, temperamenting air; the sea with its invitations; the heaven deep with worlds; and the answering brain and nervous structure replying to these; the eye that looketh into the deeps which again look back to the eye, abyss to abyss; — these, not like a glass bead, or coins or carpets, are given immeasurably to all.

"The heaven deep with worlds": the night sky, space with its emptiness and its stellar universes, but also the religious awe awakened by the imaginative presencing of this whole, this visible or imaginable aspect of the One—"the wise wonder at this mystic element of time," the "secular" and the "sacred" blended indistinguishably in the way so typical of Emerson's imagination—these feelings tell us sufficiently well why he has called the days "divine." Their divinity is ambiguous in the same way that "heaven" used as Emerson uses it here is ambiguous.

Now we are prepared for the next two sentences following the passage just quoted. "This miracle is hurled into
every beggar's hands. The blue sky [there's no need for
Emerson to say "heaven" at this point, and good reason not
to] is a covering for a market and for the cherubim and
seraphim." (Emerson felt there was no danger that his readers would flatten his poetry and destroy his meaning by taking *these* figures literally.) But if the days offer us themselves, that is, offer miracles, why in the poem do we
choose, as hungry beggars might, only "a few herbs and
apples"? What the poem fails to make clear, the prose passage does. We do not *recognize* the miraculous depth and
richness of time, we deny by our choices if not in our creeds
that time and eternity meet in an eternal now and so we
remain imprisoned in the illusions bred by common-sense
understanding. In our limited apprehension of time we
prove ourselves as unimaginative as the farmer and Bonaparte in their inadequate conception of wealth. We rou-
tinize and trivialize our days.

> Such are the days,—the earth is the cup, the sky is the
> cover, of the immense bounty of nature which is offered
> us for our daily aliment; but what force of *illusion* begins
> life with us and attends us to the end! . . . This element of
> illusion lends all its force to hide the values of present
> time. . . . An everlasting Now reigns in nature, which hangs
> the same roses on our bushes which charmed the Roman
> and the Chaldaean in their hanging gardens. 'To what end,
> then,' he asks, 'should I study languages, and traverse coun-
> tries, to learn so simple truths?'

The reason for our beggarly choice among the gifts offered
us by the days in the poem has become clearer in the poetry
of the prose, not "clearer" in some thin propositional sense
("illusion" prevents our recognizing the truly valuable gifts)
but clearer because all the meanings of the days themselves
and what they offer us for the taking have been imaginatively enriched by being both extended and deepened. We
are in a position now to understand that we have shielded

ourselves from feeling the depth of "the deep to-day," perhaps partly because we fear that if we did feel it, we should
have to recognize that "every day is Doomsday." Our illusions protect us and impoverish us at once: "One of the
illusions is that the present hour is not the critical decisive
hour." Meanwhile, "HE lurks, *he* hides,—*he* who is success,
reality, joy, and power." *Deus absconditus*. We understand
now what Emerson means when he concludes that "We owe
to genius always the same debt, of lifting the curtain from
the common, and showing us that divinities are sitting dis-
guised in the seeming gang of gypsies and pedlers."

Emerson in this meditation on the meaning of days has,
I suggest, been doing exactly the job of work he assigns to
the poet in the essay of that title, "reattaching" our days "to
nature and the Whole" and thus filling with value again
what habitude has made seem empty and trivial. If every
day is Doomsday, then the *ligaments* (Latin, *ligāre*, to bind;
religiō, the bond between man and the gods) binding the
many and the One, time and eternity, have been laid bare.
Who but a poet or prophet could do it? No wonder Emerson, knowing that this might be done, for him and for us,
goes on to confess that he holds ordinary historical scholarship in low esteem: "And him I reckon the most learned
scholar, not who can unearth for me the buried dynasties
of Sesostris and Ptolemy . . . but who can unfold the theory
of this particular Wednesday. Can he uncover the ligaments
concealed from all but piety, which attach the dull men and
things we know to the First Cause?"

It seems to me that the poetic prose of "Works and Days,"
though of course neither so concise nor so structurally tight
as the verse of "Days," and thus not so easy to hold all at
once in memory, is imaginatively richer, more widely, deeply, and complexly evocative, and so in the sense in which
poetry "means," more meaningful. Perhaps we should say
that the poem does not so much "condense" as "abstract" a
part of the argument of the essay, though to be sure it conveys its meaning through visual images. Its images make

clear the idea flatly stated in the essay as "You must treat
the days respectfully . . . ," but what in the poem persuades
us of the different sort of truth of the sentence immediately
preceding in the essay, which asserts that "life is good only
when it is magical and musical, a perfect timing and consent. . . ."? As Emerson himself first and last always insisted,
there are realms of being, realities, which only feeling and
imagination can discover. Essentially, the speaker's choice
in the poem is a prose choice, as unimaginative as the farmer's and Bonaparte's conception of wealth. Herbs and apples are pleasure-giving, tangible, useful, as owning land is,
but they are not the gifts that can lift us into transcendence.
"He only can enrich me who can recommend to me the
space between sun and sun. 'Tis the measure of a man,—his
apprehension of a day."

"There can be no greatness without abandonment,"
Emerson tells us toward the end of the essay. The statement is intended to apply to living, not to writing, but it
may be read as offering a clue to why this essay strikes me
as poetically richer than the poem. In the best of his prose
Emerson achieved a directed "abandonment," relaxing
judgment enough to allow the free play of feeling and imagination, following their leads without losing touch with fact,
riding just below the crests of their waves like an expert
surfer who has learned to relax and take advantage of his
smallness, yielding to the wave's power to ride freely toward shore. Only in the best of his poems could Emerson
feel and imagine so freely without loss of balance and
direction.

The brief poem called "The Informing Spirit" and the
opening paragraph of the essay "Circles" provide another
example of the way in which the prose often reaches levels
of poetic intensity and richness attained only in the best of
the verse, an example that while not so impressive as a comparison of "Days" and "Works and Days," has the advantage that it can be treated more briefly. Both the poem and
the prose paragraph treat the nature of the One that Emer-

son sometimes called the Over-Soul, sometimes the World-Soul, and relate that nature to our lives, but the poem strikes me as hardly more than versified argument in its first stanza and as fanciful nonsense in its second, the prose as prose-poetry of a higher order. Here is the poem:

> There is no great and no small
> To the Soul that maketh all:
> And where it cometh, all things are;
> And it cometh everywhere.
>
> I am owner of the sphere,
> Of the seven stars and the solar year,
> Of Caesar's hand, and Plato's brain,
> Of Lord Christ's heart, and Shakespeare's strain.

Now here is the opening paragraph of one of Emerson's greatest essays. It immediately evokes the metaphor that will control the whole essay, moving from that which is nearest, the eye, to that which is present but hidden from us, seemingly remote, and finally to the nature of our whole experience. Note how the rhythm becomes more pronounced as Emerson moves into his subject.

> The eye is the first circle; the horizon which it forms is the second; and throughout nature this primary figure is repeated without end. It is the highest emblem in the cipher of the world. St. Augustine described the nature of God as a circle whose centre was everywhere and its circumference nowhere. We are all our life-time reading the copious sense of this first of forms. One moral we have already deduced in considering the circular or compensatory character of every human action. Another analogy we shall now trace, that every action admits of being outdone. Our life is an apprenticeship to the truth that around every circle another can be drawn; that there is no end in nature, but every end is a beginning; and that there is always another dawn risen on mid-noon, and under every deep a lower deep opens.[10]

[10] *Works*, II, p. 281.

The poem first prosaically spells out several of the implications of the paradoxical definition of God attributed to St.
Augustine—for if the Ultimately Real is like a circle whose
center cannot be pinpointed or its circumference located,
then all such distinctions as great and small are without
meaning, and location in time and space is an illusion only;
then, in its second stanza, draws a comforting personal conclusion from this: if the center of the circle is everywhere,
it is in me too, so that "I am part and parcel of God," as
Emerson put it elsewhere, in prose, and more attractively
I should say than here in the poem, where the immunity
from contradiction offered by verse permits him to claim
ownership, and thus control, not only of the powers of
Caesar, Plato, Christ, and Shakespeare but of the "sphere"
itself. Which sphere, we wonder, the sphere of the partly
visible cosmos or the invisible sphere that is God? The
poem that begins as prosaic reasoning from a partially unstated premise becomes in its second stanza a wildly fanciful delusion of unlimited power expressed not, it would
seem, in paradoxes—though presumably the assertions
must have been so intended—but simply in statements that
seem out of touch with fact and common sense, having none
of that "veracity" that Emerson believed was the hallmark
of the finest poetry. The prose passage does not "reason" at
all but merely asserts, proceeding by "the logic of metaphor" and the method of paradox—and in it the paradoxes
work. The eye does not "form" the horizon in any common-
sense meaning of "form." A circle described as Emerson
here describes it, following his neo-Platonic teachers, would
be impossible to locate in space and so impossible to identify as a circle. If every end is a beginning, there is no common-sense meaning left in the word *end*. And so on through
the paradoxes offensive to the understanding. To the imagination habituated to paradox, on the other hand, the paragraph opens up suggestions so rich that the rest of the essay
is needed to explore them. In short, the prose paragraph
strikes me as more successfully "poetic" by Emerson's own

standards than the poem. The poem appears to be reasoning, with only the "therefores" left out; the prose paragraph
gives us metaphors whose full implications become the subject of the rest of the essay.

A final example, this time with what seems to me a much
better poem being compared with a passage of heightened
prose on the same subject. The poem and the essay, both
entitled "Illusions," show Emerson writing at a level somewhere near his best, but it seems to me that the power of
the poem is more scattered and fragmentary than that of
the final paragraph of the essay. Here is the poem:

> Flow, flow the waves hated,
> Accursed, adored,
> The waves of mutation;
> No anchorage is.
> Sleep is not, death is not;
> Who seem to die live.
> House you were born in,
> Friends of your spring-time,
> Old man and young maid,
> Day's toil and its guerdon,
> They are all vanishing,
> Fleeing to fables,
> Cannot be moored.
> See the stars through them,
> Through treacherous marbles.
> Know the stars yonder,
> The stars everlasting,
> Are fugitive also,
> And emulate, vaulted,
> The lambent heat lightning
> And fire-fly's flight.
>
> When thou dost return
> On the wave's circulation,
> Behold the shimmer,
> The wild dissipation,
> And, out of endeavor
> To change and to flow,

The gas become solid,
And phantoms and nothings
Return to be things,
And endless imbroglio
Is law and the world, —
Then first shalt thou know,
That in the wild turmoil,
Horsed on the Proteus,
Thou ridest to power,
And to endurance.

Here is the conclusion of the essay of which the poem
serves as a "motto." Notice how, as in the paragraph from
"Circles," the rhythm of the prose changes, grows, mounts
to a climax, whereas the rhythm of the poem is static and
the climax depends for whatever power it has on flat prose
assertion, an assertion which the falling effect of the ca-
dence seems not only not to support but to contradict. The
final words of the prose passage, which Emerson had first
found in his translation of Plotinus and which he used over
and over because they struck him as a revelation of the essential nature of religious experience, are not so much a logical conclusion from what precedes as a thoroughly prepared imaginative leap into the unknown.

> There is no chance and no anarchy in the universe. All
> is system and gradation. Every god is there sitting in his
> sphere. The young mortal enters the hall of the firmament;
> there is he alone with them alone, they pouring on him
> benedictions and gifts, and beckoning him up to their
> thrones. On the instant, and incessantly, fall snow-storms
> of illusions. He fancies himself in a vast crowd which sways
> this way and that and whose movement and doings he must
> obey: he fancies himself poor, orphaned, insignificant. The
> mad crowd drives hither and thither, now furiously com-
> manding this thing to be done, now that. What is he that
> he should resist their will, and think or act for himself?
> Every moment new changes and new showers of deceptions
> to baffle and distract him. And when, by and by, for an

instant, the air clears and the cloud lifts a little, there are
the gods still sitting around him on their thrones, — they
alone with him alone.[11]

Up to this point I have tried to illustrate the poetic effects
of Emerson's prose chiefly by drawing on the less well-
known essays, which possess the advantage that we can approach them more attentively, with fewer preconceptions.
But I should not want to conclude without mentioning any
of the more famous essays. Here are two examples, then, the
first from "The Poet," one of the most impassioned and
imaginative early essays, which, not by chance as I see it,
has also struck many of Emerson's readers as one of the
most profoundly meaningful. The last paragraph of the essay is a great Romantic prose-poem on the nature, the
destiny, and the ultimate power of the poet who becomes
the true Namer and Sayer for his age and his people. We
must *hear* the words, reading them slowly, solemnly, as
though they were lines in bardic poetry:

> O poet! a new nobility is conferred in groves and pas-
> tures, and not in castles or by the sword-blade any longer.
> The conditions are hard, but equal. Thou shalt leave the
> world, and know the muse only. Thou shalt not know any
> longer the times, customs, graces, politics, or opinions of
> men, but shalt take all from the muse. For the time of towns
> is tolled from the world by funeral chimes, but in nature
> the universal hours are counted by succeeding tribes of ani-
> mals and plants, and by growth of joy on joy. God wills
> also that thou abdicate a manifold and duplex life, and
> that thou be content that others speak for thee. Others
> shall be thy gentlemen and shall represent all courtesy and
> worldly life for thee; others shall do the great and resound-
> ing actions also. Thou shalt lie close hid with nature, and
> canst not be afforded to the Capitol or the Exchange. The
> world is full of renunciations and apprenticeships, and
> this is thine; thou must pass for a fool and a churl for a
> long season. This is the screen and sheath in which Pan

[11] *The Conduct of Life, Works,* VI, p. 308.

has protected his well-beloved flower, and thou shalt be
known only to thine own, and they shall console thee with
tenderest love. And thou shalt not be able to rehearse the
names of thy friends in thy verse, for an old shame before
the holy ideal. And this is the reward; that the ideal shall
be real to thee, and the impressions of the actual world
shall fall like summer rain, copious, but not troublesome
to thy invulnerable essence. Thou shalt have the whole
land for thy park and manor, the sea for thy bath and
navigation, without tax and without envy; the woods and
the rivers thou shalt own, and thou shalt possess that where-
in others are only tenants and boarders. Thou true land-
lord! sea-lord! Wherever snow falls or water flows or birds
fly, wherever day and night meet in twilight, wherever the
blue heaven is hung by clouds or sown with stars, wherever
are forms with transparent boundaries, wherever are outlets
into celestial space, wherever is danger, and awe, and love,
— there is Beauty, plenteous as rain, shed for thee, and
though thou shouldst walk the world over, thou shalt not
be able to find a condition inopportune or ignoble.

All of Emerson's ideas about how prose might be so written as to move us to assent are here illustrated, along with
others that anyone who had studied Blair's *Rhetoric* as
Emerson had would have been familiar with even if he did
not think it necessary to state them. "Iterations of phrase"
are the kind of rhyme suitable to prose: "Thou shalt leave
the world. . . . Thou shalt not know. . . . Thou shalt lie close.
. . . And thou shalt not be able. . . ." And another "trope"
emphasized by Blair, "iteration" of sound alone: "For the
*t*ime of the *t*owns is *t*olled . . . ," and so on, all the way
through. "Put the argument into a concrete shape, into an
image. . . ." And, as Emerson did not counsel but so often
practiced, let your argument rest on and develop paradox:
the poet's way to power lies in abdication and renunciation,
and the wealth that is his reward can be neither counted
nor measured. The final sentence, beginning "Wherever
snow falls or water flows or birds fly," deserves to be read
once again, this time with no thought at all of the "argu-

ment" just inadequately paraphrased but with the inner ear
open to the cadences that support and extend it. It might
be difficult to show that any of the passages of "Song of Myself" that describe the poet contain more moving and beautiful poetry than this prose rapture.

The other example I am allowing myself, the ending of
"Experience," is less likely to seem persuasive in brief quotation, for here the prose is not obviously heightened as it
is in the peroration of "The Poet." But the very plainness of
the style is my reason for choosing it, even though for a full
appreciation of the point I want to make the reader may
have to reread the whole essay. "Experience" is describable
as an expository essay, but I would suggest that the experiment of reading it as a prose poem is likely to increase our
respect for it. As in any poem of considerable length, its sec-
tions vary in imaginative intensity, some parts being merely
explanatory or transitional. The body of the essay is devoted to describing and evoking, often in the most brilliant
metaphors, all those aspects of our experience that baffle
and deceive us, making certainty elude us, draining all reality from an experience that still, as in a dream, remains
vivid with the vividness of a hallucination. Yet at the end
of the essay there is a low-keyed note of reassurance: "Patience and patience, we shall win at the last." As I read it,
the affirmation does not ring hollow or appear in the least
forced, but to see how it can seem inevitable after so long
and moving an enumeration of all that frustrates us, we
shall have to recall the way the essay begins. The imagery
of the opening sentences evokes a sense of the paradoxes we
become aware of when we attempt to locate ourselves in
time and space, to understand the gross sensible reality of
our lives:

> Where do we find ourselves? In a series of which we do
> not know the extremes, and believe that it has none. We
> wake and find ourselves on a stair; there are stairs below
> us, which we seem to have ascended; there are stairs above
> us, many a one, which go upward and out of sight. But the

Genius which according to the old belief stands at the
door by which we enter, and gives us the lethe to drink,
that we may tell no tales, mixed the cup too strongly, and
we cannot shake off the lethargy now at noonday. Sleep
lingers all our lifetime about our eyes, as night hovers all
day in the boughs of the fir-tree. All things swim and glitter.
Our life is not so much threatened as our perception.
Ghostlike we glide through nature, and should not know
our place again.[12]

The affirmation at the end is achieved by a shift of perspective, by changing the angle of our vision, or, in equally
Emersonian terms, by rising to that higher level of perception attainable, paradoxically, only when we cease attempting to penetrate by our understanding the deceptions of the
space-time world. Notice how Emerson makes his point in
his closing sentences by naming concretely some of those
seeming-solid routine activities that by now have been
emptied of reality, and then contrasting them with the "sanity and revelations" not of more substantial facts and arguments but of the heart's dream of "true romance" and "victory," persistent aspirations that turn out to be more
dependable clues to reality than the heartiest dinner. The
style here could hardly be more unlike that of the closing
of "The Poet." It is straightforward, unadorned, at first
literal and then openly hortatory. Its effectiveness as
"poetry" springs at once from its closeness to fact, both the
outward facts of eating and sleeping and the inward "facts"
of the heart's motions, and from its paradoxical relation to
all that has preceded it as it picks up and repeats in a new
key the words and images that have run all through the
essay—time, sleep, forgetting; sight, insight, power:

We must be very suspicious of the deceptions of the element
of time. It takes a good deal of time to eat or to sleep, or
to earn a hundred dollars, and a very little time to enter-
tain a hope and an insight which becomes the light of our
life. We dress our garden, eat our dinners, discuss the house-

[12] *Works*, III, p. 49.

hold with our wives, and these things make no impression, are forgotten next week; but, in the solitude to which every man is always returning, he has a sanity and revelations which in his passage into new worlds he will carry with him. Never mind the ridicule, never mind the defeat; up again, old heart! — it seems to say, — there is victory yet for all justice; and the true romance which the world exists to realize will be the transformation of genius into practical power.[13]

It is increasingly common to encounter praise of Emerson's intelligence coupled with the admission or warning that the intelligence does not reveal itself in his public works, certainly not in the better-known essays, only in the Journal. The position seems to me to reflect two confusions, a confusion about what "intelligence" is and about the various ways in which it may manifest itself, and a confusion about what the essays are and, since they *are* what they are, how they ought to be read.

To take up the second confusion first, the essays are not logical or philosophical treatises and should not be so read. If we read them as straightforward theoretical expositions of subjects also treated by theologians, philosophers, and social scientists, they generally fail us miserably. In the early essays especially, we may search in vain even for a theoretically adequate formulation of the problems to be treated, and the treatment of the problems is nearly always one-sided, oversimplified, and ambiguous, often all these at the same time. Discovering in himself very early no talent for logical argument, only a gift for using words, Emerson wisely resolved never to argue, and he kept to his resolve in both his personal associations and his writings. Confronted with a contrary opinion, even one backed by contrary evidence, he merely smiled and kept his conviction. Despite the respect in which—quite correctly, as I see it—

[13] *Ibid.*, pp. 85-86.

James, Santayana, and Dewey held him, he was neither a
competent theologian nor a competent philosopher in the
usual modern senses of those words, and he himself knew
it very well. When his essays now and then give the appearance of close reasoning, the appearance is almost always
deceptive; when it is not, an examination of the logical
structure of the reasoning, and particularly of the *lacunae*
in it, will quickly reveal its inadequacies.

The best of the essays are not then theoretic expositions
but poetic, and at their best often paradoxical, meditations.
They were so intended and should be so read. When they
are read as what they are, they offer us many of the rewards poetry offers us, though to be sure in a less concentrated form, except for a brief passage here and there. It
must be clear by this time that in saying this I do not mean
to imply that they have no "knowledge-value," that they
offer only "emotive" satisfactions. Failing us as propositional theory, they may still do for us what we expect poetry to do, to make such use of all the expressive powers of
language and the thought-provoking powers of paradox
that they refresh and extend those powers and so stimulate,
refresh, and enlarge our ability to feel, to imagine, and to
think. Nourishing, as poetry does, these psychological activities—"psychological" as contrasted with biological and social—the essays can liberate and enrich us, making us more
distinctively human.

Like the poems, to be sure, the essays are primarily
"thoughtful," not primarily "imaginative" in the sense in
which editors of literary anthologies once grouped poetry,
fiction, and drama under the heading "imaginative literature"—leaving the impression that *Walden* must be unimaginative; and they are certainly not markedly sensuous.
But if they are not "imaginative" in the old limited definition, they are imaginative to the core in a deeper and better
one. They are "visionary" in both the literal and the figurative sense, for the valuable core of them is a compound of
what an extraordinarily intelligent man has seen, has ob-

served *with* the eye, with the insights achieved by looking not with but through the eye;[14] and both types of vision move back and forth between the outward and the inward worlds, pausing longest usually to focus on the area of the conjunction of the two worlds where inner and outer, subjective and objective meet and coexist in paradox. Observations form the core of the essays, observations that alternately lead to and follow from what look like propositions but usually turn out to be more simulated than real propositions, propositions offensive to common sense. Self-reliance is God-reliance. "Books are for the scholar's idle times." The passing moment contains eternity. The intangible is more real than the tangible. The greatest self-realization comes by self-abandonment. These are paradoxes, word-plays and thought-plays at once, aimed at shocking us into taking a fresh look at ourselves and our experience and then reconceiving them.

The best of the essays are the prose-poems of a skeptical religious seeker and visionary recording what he has seen both with and through the eye, the often discordant results of sight and insight; noting the discrepancies and searching for the correspondences, then going on from there to imagine the cosmos, the ultimate elusive unity of the One, the whole; and wishing for and imagining freedom, power, and meaning in it; "fantasizing," we might almost say, about the richness of human experience and power in a meaningful cosmos.

Imagination, fantasy, wishful thinking—these are not three wholly distinct activities, the first associated with artists and creativity, the second primarily in our minds with

14 In "Poetry and Imagination" Emerson illustrates his discussion of the relations between sight and insight by quoting with approval a passage from Blake beginning "He who does not imagine in stronger and better lineaments and in stronger and better light than his perishing mortal eye can see, does not imagine at all" and ending by saying of the "corporeal eye," "I look through it, and not with it." (*Works*, VIII, pp. 31-32.)

sex, the third with objectively unsound thinking, but in essence three manifestations of one activity. The activity may
deceive, or be a substitute for actions and so deserve to be
called "neurotic fantasy," or it may uncover or discover
truth or reality, existing or yet to be created, in which case
we call it imagination. But the thinking in Emerson's essays
is often—at its best, I should say usually—not just "imaginative" but "wishful," but not wishful in the sense of idle day-
dreams whose only function is to serve as a substitute for
the impossible or forbidden deed, wishful rather in the
sense of giving symbolic expression in words to dreams of
possibilities beyond the conventional and the trivial and
shallow. The thinking in the essays is sometimes shrewd and
"realistic," to be sure, but when it is most imaginative it is
most likely to be "wishful" in this sense. What, if not wish,
would prompt thinking to dwell so persistently on unreal-
ized ideal possibilities that seem incapable of realization
and then invite us to try to realize them in action?

The essays (and of course the poems too) were the form
of "action" for which Emerson felt himself uniquely suited.
The poet could leave detailed knowledge of fact to the scientists and ordinary logic to the philosophers, to the "knowers," and leave "great and resounding actions" to the men
of action, the "doers." Words were the poet's province,
whether he wrote in verse or in prose; and though his
words could not lay claim to the purity or exactness of the
knowledge achieved by the Knowers, or the immediate
public impact of the deeds of the Doers, and so required of
him renunciations, he could work on in the faith that insofar
as his were the right words, they would have their effect on
the feeling, the imagining, the dreaming, and even the
thinking of other men, and so in the end help to reshape the
world more exactly known by the scientist and more immediately influenced by the man of action.

Insofar then as the essays can still move and enlighten us,
they do so because of the way Emerson chose and arranged
the words that compose them. That they are neither orig-

inal nor even coherent as philosophy, that if we read them
as theoretic treatments of the problems they discuss we find
them deficient even in the most elementary sense, that is,
inadequately aware of the relevant data, has little or nothing to do with their real value, as Santayana in effect
pointed out long ago. Emerson himself said all that really
needs to be said about how to read his best essays and what
their value for us is. "Imaginative minds cling to their
images. . . . A happy symbol is a sort of evidence that your
thought is just. . . . The poet has a logic, though it be
subtile. . . . There is no more welcome gift to men than a
new symbol."[15] As imaginative symbolizations, as prose
poems that rely heavily for their impact and their meaning
on their imagery, their rhythms and "iterations," and their
paradoxical affronts to common sense, the best of the essays
are works of art capable of enlarging and enriching the
reality we creatively discover, and then inhabit, as truly
works of art in their own way as *The Scarlet Letter* and
Moby-Dick are.

[15] "Poetry and Imagination," *Works*, VIII, pp. 17-19, 26.

CHAPTER V

Vision and Voice

If Emerson had been alive to read James's review of Cabot's *Memoir*, with its combination of high praise for the man and his work and its doubt that the writings could really be said to have been "composed," he might have smiled and, realizing that it was not so intended, have taken James's qualification as a compliment anyway, for had he not always said that mere compositional skill could not give a writer greatness? Today we are likely to feel that both Emerson's Platonism—all poetry was written before time was—and James's formalism—style is everything—are equally one-sided apprehensions of a complex reality, so that Emerson's continuing to seem important as a writer does not puzzle us so much as it did James, even while the problem James first isolated continues to seem to be a problem in all but the best of Emerson's poetry in verse. If a writer's finding his form means mastering an appropriate form, then Emerson did surely, as Chapman first argued, find his form in the lecture-essay. As a prose-poet in his essays, Emerson was a master stylist, fully in control whenever he wrote, not just in rare moments of unusual inspiration. Regarding the prose, I think we must conclude that James was simply wrong.

But of course we ought to remember if we say this that there was nothing essentially novel, nothing experimental about the style of Emerson's prose, even about his most poetic prose. It was produced at a time when High Rhetoric was much admired. True, in various subtle ways Emerson's prose style bore the stamp of his personality and situation. Even in its rhetorical flights it is distinguishable from the eloquent rhetoric of Macaulay, Carlyle, or Ruskin. Still, though sufficiently personal in the voice we hear in it, it makes no fundamental break with the prose conventions of

the age. Its tropes and devices are all to be found defined
and illustrated in Blair's *Rhetoric*, which Emerson had
studied and absorbed in college. Though Emerson gave
command of the subject and novelty of content priority
over rhetorical devices in his late essay "Eloquence," his
best essays fully illustrate the rhetorical devices he largely
took for granted in his discussion of how to hold and persuade an audience—or readers, if the lectures became essays, as they normally did.

Our own age has grown a little suspicious of the high
rhetorical style, wanting, as Emerson himself did, truth, not
manipulation, from words. It may well be then that especially for younger readers the functional beauty and power
of Emerson's prose-poetry is harder to appreciate than the
power of the "rough," halting, often apparently fumbling
poems that make up the bulk of his writing in verse form.
But for his own age it was quite otherwise. Wholly prepared to be moved by the poetry of the prose, readers
found the bulk of the verse disappointing their every expec-
tation about what poems should be like. No wonder Emerson's influence on his own age was mediated chiefly through
his lectures and essays.

When readers in Emerson's time found his prose finely "poetic" and the verse, for the most part, lamentably "prosaic,"
they were making a value judgment which we are unlikely
to accept, unless we have read no poetry since Longfellow's
and Tennyson's, but their judgment contains a kind of truth
of fact if not of value. Emerson wrote his verse, as we have
seen, in a variety of styles, one of which was not only conventional in his time but even conservative, slightly old-
fashioned by the time it was published. A modification of
the style of the pre-Romantic Graveyard Poets, this style
gave no offense and offered no surprises. His occasional use
of blank verse, too, was conventional enough, except in the
opening lines of "Hamatreya," to satisfy prevailing concep-

tions of the properly "poetic." But much of his verse, the bulk of it indeed, was poetry of a kind his age could not easily recognize as "poetic."

Its style was, I should say, agreeing with Strauch and Yoder, "experimental." Those aspects of it which struck his age as "harsh," "rough," tuneless or unmelodious may be taken as signs that he was experimentally attempting to put into practice ideas—changing ideas at that, which made his problem all the greater—about a different kind of poetry from the pretty "magazine verses" his age so much admired and he tended to despise, verses which showed "talent" only, he thought, not inspiration or genius. The irregularity of his meters, his movement at times away from any recognizable accentual-syllabic meter into what I have described as his dipodic rhythms, the casualness and irregularity of his rhyming, his tendency to shift from one recognized form to another in the same poem—all this and more led most of his nineteenth-century critics and a good many of their followers in the early decades of this century to conclude that Emerson, though he had the "soul" of a poet and could occasionally, apparently by happy accident, compose conventional poetic melodies, unfortunately had no "ear" for the music of verse. Emerson himself at times seemed to lend his support to this view, as in the statement quoted by his son in his notes to the Centenary Edition of the *Poems*: "I think sometimes that my lack of musical ear is made good to me through my eyes: that which others hear I see."

But I find no reason to believe that Emerson had a deficient "ear" for the sound of verse. Apart from the fact that much of his youthful verse was "melodious" enough, there are several other reasons for believing that the opinion that he had no poetic "ear" must be rejected. First, while it seems to be true that Emerson had little experience or knowledge of, and apparently limited appreciation of, music—that is, literal music, as in the phrase "the music of Beethoven"—that fact, if it is one, cannot be used to explain the "roughness" of much of his mature verse. As Eliot's essay "The Music of Poetry" has made clear once and for all, I would hope, the "music" of poetry and the "music" of music are analogous but very far from being identical. To have an ear for "the music of poetry" is to be sensitive to the discrete sounds, patterns of repetition, and cadences of *language*, that is, of verbal speech. It is highly unlikely that a man as sensitive to the sound-values of language—as for example they are found in heightened or "poetic" prose—as Emerson obviously was would be "tone-deaf" to the sound of language arranged in verse patterns. No single feature of the "music" of poetry is peculiar to verse alone. Its "music" represents a formalized heightening, intensifying, of the sound-values found not only in "poetic prose," of which Emerson produced a great deal, but in ordinary speech patterns ("the sound of sense," Robert Frost would call it) and in cries of sorrow and joy, in lamentations, prayers, spells, and the like.

Another consideration: how did it happen that Emerson, not only in his youth but all through his creative life, could write *some* poems that no reader has ever found deficient in "music," if he lacked an "ear" for poetic "music"? No one has ever complained of a deficiency of "music" in "The Concord Hymn" or a number of other poems of his maturity.

More could be said, but enough. The allegation that he lacked an "ear" for the "music" of verse rests on a fundamental confusion of two distinct art forms and is thus either a meaningless or an erroneous statement. In "Poetry and Imagination" Emerson remarked that among his favorite poems, there were some that he recalled by remembering how they *sounded*, as of course a man seriously lacking in sensitivity to the sound of verse would not, and possibly could not.[1]

Still, after we have rejected both Victorian ideas of the kind of "music" verse must have and the favorite Victorian explanation for the failure of his verse to have it; after we

[1] *Works*, VIII, p. 52.

have admitted that he wrote in several, not just one, style and that the man who described himself as a "seeker" in life may be recognized by us as an experimenter in verse; after all this and more that might be said *contra* both Victorian and New Critical rejections of the verse, James's judgment that he was a writer who had not found but was seeking his form comes back, not argued away but still seeming to need to be reckoned with.

I am not sure I know what James meant, or one should mean, by saying that a writer has not "found his form," but if we take it to mean that a writer who has found his form has "mastered," and can normally produce more or less at will, a style wholly suited to his purposes, I believe we shall have to decide that as a poet in verse Emerson never really "mastered," though he quite often achieved, a style adequate to the expression of his vision. Here we are back again, of course, with the rival ideas of poetry as composition and poetry as condensed memorable truth-speaking. Clearly there is a sense in which each emphasis needs the other to complete it.

Not long before his death in 1973, W. H. Auden, by then the "dean" of the great Modernist poets, stated succinctly what he believed we "demand" of a poem, what we expect to find in a poem we judge successful:

> One demands two things of a poem. Firstly, it must be a well-made verbal object that does honor to the language in which it is written. Secondly, it must say something significant about a reality common to us all, but perceived from a unique perspective. What the poet says has never been said before, but, once he has said it, his readers recognize its validity for themselves.[2]

In short, the poem as a "composed" verbal artifact and the poem as a perception. I doubt that when we personally respond to a poem we do so in terms of this dichotomy, which

2 "The Poems of Joseph Brodsky," *The New York Review of Books,* 20:5 (April 5, 1973), 10.

seems to imply, first, that we either "know the rules" in terms of which a poem may be considered "well-made" or have an "aesthetic faculty" quite distinct from our sense of truth and reality, and second that, similarly, we can judge the validity for us of a poetic perception without regard to how it is stated. The end result of the first idea, if it were true, would be aestheticism, of the second, "message-hunting."

But if we respond to, experience, poems in a unitary, not a dichotomous way, we can still stand back and discuss them in terms that assume that form and content are separable—as indeed they are in some respects, for some purposes, in all but the completely successful poem. The form is good—for what? The idea, the truth, the perception that is struggling for expression—how does it get expressed, how much do we have to guess at it from knowing the author's other works or his stated intentions or the unexamined, unexpressed assumptions of the age? Just as we often can guess the intention of a stammerer even though some of the words remain unuttered or unintelligible, so we often say of the graceful and polished utterance that it is trivial or empty. So, though Auden's statement of the two demands we make of a poem appears to raise the old form-content problem in a way that implies the falsity, or at least only the partial truth, of Emerson's organicist idea that form and content are inseparable—an idea that the New Critics also insisted upon, of course—nevertheless I think we can and should accept it as a common-sense statement of what we do indeed "demand" of a poem, even if it does some violence to the way we experience a poem that appeals to us and that we judge to be excellently written.

So we ask again, did Emerson as a poet master a verse style? To say that he was an experimenter does not at all imply a positive answer to this, even though it amounts to a kind of praise. After an experimeter has succeeded in achieving the aim of his experiments, he stops experimenting—unless of course his ideas about what he wants to

achieve have changed, so that he must start experimenting
again. By Auden's first compositional yardstick, Emerson
wrote many fine and some great poems, but he did not
"master a style," for many of the "experimental" features of
his style that work so well in the best poems work very ill
indeed in the poorest. His unconventional use of rhyme is
a case in point: if my discussion of it in the preceding chapter is at all convincing, his rhyming in some of his poorer
poems often seems forced and sometimes more than a little
absurd, as well as expressive of an ill-founded confidence
in his ability to decipher the "correspondences" between
nature and spirit; or else it seems in conflict with his own
fundamentally Heraclitean vision of nature as unceasing
flow.

One might be tempted at this point to say that if Emerson
did not master a style in verse, he did in the poetry of his
prose, which surely passes Auden's first test, that of the
"well-made verbal object." But we cannot take this line
without denying the validity of Emerson's own lifelong
ideas about the relations of poetry and prose, ideas that
were perfectly traditional in holding that poetry (verse, that
is) is the "higher" art form. So that by Emerson's own standard, if as a poet he found his form only, or even best, in
prose, then James's impression that he had not found his
form retains at least partial validity.

But enough of such considerations and reconsiderations.
No critic has ever yet praised Emerson as consistently a
master craftsman in verse, and I can't imagine any critic
doing so soon. Auden's first demand—and James's similar,
though only implied, standard—should be satisfied if Emerson wrote a sufficient number of poems that seem to us well-
written, even if he never did fully "master" a verse style.
What then about his perceptions, his vision?

Here too I think we can find no easy answers. A remark
that Frost is said to have made to his friend Robert Francis
in 1934 may serve to open up the subject. Frost, we recall,
considered that Emerson could be described as a "philo-

sophical poet" or a "poetic philosopher"—his favorite kind
of both, he added—but in the conversation Francis reports,
though it is clear to Francis that Emerson is for Frost
"America's greatest poet," Frost warns that we must, in
Francis' paraphrase of Frost's meaning, watch out for "the
flaws in his thinking." "The half-gods do not go," Francis
tells us Frost said by way of illustration,[3] referring, of
course, to Emerson's concluding lines in "Give All to Love,"
"When half-gods go, / The gods arrive." Frost is quite right,
I think: it would make life so much simpler, I suppose, if
the half-gods would go, but they don't—as Emerson himself
came more and more to realize with the passing years, as
he moved gradually from his early Transcendentalism to
the transcendental theism of "Works and Days."

One wonders whether Frost ever pondered the question
of how Emerson could be at once America's greatest poet
and a philosophical poet whose ideas (philosophy) were
often faulty. Whether Frost did or not, we must. "Give All
to Love" is written in Emerson's characteristic "experimental" style with lines of varying length, mostly short, no consistent metrical pattern, and irregular rhyme, but it strikes
me as a most unsatisfactory poem by the yardstick of
Auden's second demand: its way of perceiving reality does
not fit mine at all, so the poem is not "true" for me. Emerson's "vision" in this poem seems to me faulty, so though the
poem is well enough composed, the style cannot save it as
a poem.

There were several subjects, aspects of "our common
reality," on which Emerson could not think-feel-imagine
well and so could not write well. The most eloquent voice
cannot—I think should not be allowed to—persuade us of
the truth of a faulty vision. To certain most important aspects of experience Emerson as seer was in effect blind.
Love was one of them, grief another, the two related of
course. "Give All to Love" is as bad a poem as his essay

[3] Robert Francis, *Frost: A Time to Talk*, Amherst, The University
of Massachusetts Press, 1972, p. 70.

"Love" is bad as an essay. The essays on friendship and love
do not persuade us that he had ever deeply experienced
either friendship or love. They Platonize both experiences
and confuse them. Emerson *had* experienced love, but he
armored himself so well against the grief of Edward's
death, Ellen's death, Waldo's death, that after that he could
not afford to think about love with all the power of his mind
and heart as he could think about most other subjects. "The
Titmouse," which says we must face death with courage, is
for me a far greater poem—that is, more consonant with my
perceptions of our common reality—than "Give All to
Love." But it was not only in his later, more subdued and
stoic phase that Emerson could think and write well. The
early essay "Self-Reliance," one-sided as it is, has far more
to say to us than the later "Tragedy," which is merely con-
scientious in admitting the reality of a subject Emerson had
not treated before and had nothing new to say about. The
early poem "Uriel" is so much greater than the late poem
"My Garden" that there is simply no way of comparing
them.

Community, friendship, love, grief, tragedy—these are
all effectively absent from or effectively distorted in Emerson's vision, and together they encompass no insignificant
slice of human experience. To admit that on these subjects
Emerson really had nothing significant to say to us is certainly severely to qualify any claim that may be made for
his greatness as a poet. But I suppose we do not demand of
any poet, any artist, that he be equally strong on all subjects. Grant Emerson his subjects—especially the gods
alone, with him alone—and he may still seem one of our
major poets, despite his severe limitations, though not, in
my opinion, what Frost would have him, our best. I call him
"major" because, judging by Auden's two-fold test, I find
that he wrote a sufficiently large number of poems in distinguished verse and many beautiful prose-poems that "say
something significant about a reality common to us all, but
perceived from a unique perspective." What he said about

the subjects on which he could think and feel and imagine well had "never been said before," to use Auden's words, partly because, as Santayana believed, they had never been said as well, partly because, to return to Auden, they convey perceptions gained from a unique perspective.

Though Emerson the poet could write well on many subjects, including the evils of politics and trade, he wrote best on what was closest to his heart, seeking out the traces in experience of the fugitive gods, to return to the words of Heidegger with which I began. When he wrote on this subject in any of its aspects, affirmative as "Merlin" is, reflective as "Monadnoc" is, or cautionary as "The Titmouse" is, he often wrote strong, wholly memorable poems that say what had never been said before and that no poet has said better since. For him, staying on the track of the fugitive gods might require deflating humanism, as he does in "Limits" and "Water," or mocking the understanding, as he does in "Brahma," or reminding man of his mortality, as he does in "Hamatreya."

When I try to go beyond such limited descriptions of the meaning of particular poems of Emerson that have impressed me, I find myself remembering a statement attributed to Erich Heller that seems to characterize the general meaning of his poetry that made it important to such diverse later poets as Robinson, Frost, and A. R. Ammons:

> What is it, then, that poetry means? Its meaning is the vindication of the worth and value of the world, of life, and of human experience.[4]

[4] As quoted by Ruth Whitman in "Teaching the Sources of Poetry" [by "sources," the author means the sources within the poet himself], *The American Poetry Review*, 2:2 (March/April, 1973), 51.

Index

Eliot, T.S., 6, 46, 64, 141, 161,
194-195
Emerson (Miles), 48
*Emerson, A Collection of Critical
Essays* (Konvitz and Whicher),
53
"Emerson Among the Poets"
(Sanborn), 12, 16, 24
Emerson and Asia, 48
Emerson and Other Essays
(Chapman), 19, 21-23, 172
"Emerson and the Bardic Tradi-
tion," 49, 139-140
Emerson: An Organic Anthology
(Whicher), 46-48
Emerson As a Poet (Benton), 24
Emerson as lecturer, 15, 19
Emerson as philosopher, xii, 22,
53, 54-55, 57-58, 60-63, 80, 187-
188, 199-200
Emerson, Edward, 77, 80, 82, 88,
118, 200
Emerson, Ellen, 97, 98, 99, 139,
149, 200
Emerson Handbook, 48, 77
Emerson, Lidian, 78, 79
Emerson on the Soul, 48
Emerson: Poet and Thinker
(Carey), 28-29
Emerson, R.W., works treated
or mentioned: *Journals and
Miscellaneous Notebooks, The*,
75-107 and *passim*
Poems, "The Adirondacs,"
76, 109, "Alphonso of Castile,"
136, "Bacchus," 108, 110, 119,
135, 138, 142-146, 148, 157,
"Beauty," 163, "Blight," 111,
136, "The Bohemian Hymn,"
136, 158, "Boston," 103, "The
Boston Hymn," 103, 135, 136,
"Brahma," 71, 103, 109, 135,
155-160, 201, "Circles," 136,
"The Concord Hymn," 30, 34,

103, 110, 136, 195, "Cosmos,"
136, "Days," 46, 109, 128, 135,
136, 172-173, 175, 176, 177-178,
"Destiny" 120, 121, 127-132,
"Each and All," 28, 99, 108,
135, 136, "Fragments on Nature and Life," 136, "Give All
to Love," 199, 200, "Good-
bye," 90, 93, 99, 100, 108, 111,
118, "Grace," 136, "Hama-
treya," 46, 72, 109, 128, 135,
146-155, 157, 193, 201, "The
Humble-Bee," 120, 121-122,
132-134, 147, "Illusions," 181-
182, "The Informing Spirit,"
178-181, "A Letter," 100-101,
108, "Limits," 136, 201, "May-
Day," 118, 147, 148, 166, *May-
Day and Other Pieces*, 109,
135, "Merlin," 67, 85, 108, 118,
135, 138-142, 157, 201, "The
Miracle," 136, "Mithridates,"
136, "Monadnoc," 10, 135, 136,
201, "Monadnoc from Afar,"
136, "Music," 136, "My Garden," 164, 200, "Nahant,"
136, "Ode Inscribed to W.H.
Channing," 136, 171, *Poems*
(1847), 16-17, 63, 97, 106-107,
120, 135, *Poems* (Centenary
Edition), 118, 194, "The Problem," 28, 99, 108, 135, 136,
"The Rhodora," 135, 136,
Selected Poems, 76, "The Snow-
Storm," 105, 135, 136, "The
Sphinx," 103, 118-120, 136,
"Terminus," 109, 135, 136,
"Threnody," 34, 135, 136,
"The Titmouse," 109, 135, 136,
200, 201, "To Ellen," 97, 98-
99, "To Ellen at the South,"
97-98, "Two Rivers," 150, 171,
"Uriel," 71, 103, 128, 135, 136-
138, 200, "Water," 136, 201,

Library of Congress Cataloging in Publication Data

Waggoner, Hyatt Howe.
  Emerson as poet.

  Includes bibliographical references.
  1. Emerson, Ralph Waldo, 1803-1882—Criticism and interpretation.
I. Title.
PS1638.W3   811'.3   74-2983
ISBN 0-691-06269-2

DATE DUE

Demco, Inc. 38-293